IN THE KITCHEN

IN THE KITCHEN

Compiled by Anna Hunter

Foreword by HRH The Princess Margaret,
Countess of Snowdon

A GRAHAM TARRANT BOOK

DAVID & CHARLES
Newton Abbot   London   North Pomfret (Vt)

Acknowledgements
The publisher and the NSPCC gratefully
acknowledge the following: Glen Baxter's
illustrations by kind permission of the Nigel
Greenwood Gallery; Maurice Dodd's 'The
Perishers', John Burns' 'Jane' and Reg Smythe's
'Andy Capp' by courtesy of the *Daily Mirror*; Haro
Hodson's illustrations by courtesy of the *Daily
Mail*.

Illustrations at the beginning of each section by
William Rushton.

**British Library Cataloguing in Publication
Data**
Star turns in the kitchen – (A Graham
   Tarrant book).
   I. Food – Recipes
   1. Hunter, Anna
   641.5

ISBN 0-7153-9258-1

© NSPCC 1988

Typeset by Typesetters (Birmingham) Ltd,
Smethwick, West Midlands

Printed in Great Britain by
Butler & Tanner Ltd, Frome and London

for David & Charles Publishers plc
Brunel House   Newton Abbot   Devon

Published in the United States of America
by David & Charles Inc
North Pomfret   Vermont 05053 USA

The NSPCC gratefully acknowledges
the generous support of all
the contributors who together
have made this book possible.

CONTENTS

Most children live and grow up in loving and caring families. The cloud of abuse and neglect does not hang over them. However, for those children who face either physical, emotional or sexual abuse or neglect, a happy and carefree childhood can be something unknown.

Throughout its long history the NSPCC has worked and campaigned tirelessly for the sake of children such as these. And the Society's efforts continue today in the harsh realities of modern life.

I have been most encouraged by the magnificent response to the plight of abused children shown by countless supporters and well-wishers throughout the British Isles.

These children desperately need the NSPCC, and the NSPCC too, needs our continued support for without it, many children would go on suffering without hope.

Margaret

President, National Society for the
Prevention of Cruelty to Children

9

INTRODUCTION

It comes as no surprise in this day and age to learn that famous people, often leading incredibly busy lives, actually find time to cook for themselves and for others. Or that men (or some of them at any rate) enjoy the activity as much as most women do. But what is fun to discover, apart from the recipes themselves, is who likes what – or rather, who likes cooking what. In other words, putting a familiar face to the recipe.

Sometimes the two go naturally together. For example, roly-poly Russell Grant and Steak & Kidney Pud or the lissom Susan Hampshire and Girls' Summer Salad seem made for each other. 'Peasant Potatoes', on the other hand, is hardly a dish you would associate with the extravagant lifestyle of *Dynasty* super-star Joan Collins (unless you had first read the ingredients!); and who would guess there was room in the spartan régime of champion athlete Steve Ovett for the deliciously rich Spicy Buttermilk Coffee Cake. But then good cooks are full of surprises.

This collection of recipes, tips, culinary anecdotes and cartoon illustrations began as a result of my association with the Elstree branch of the NSPCC. At a meeting in 1987 it was suggested that we produce an NSPCC Elstree cookbook, based on recipes used for our consistently excellent Annual Ladies' Luncheon. We soon found, however, that with celebrities known to the committee and through the generosity of others we approached that there was enough material for this – a much expanded and altogether more exciting book. It seemed that the magic letters NSPCC were enough to ensure replies, from the most culinary inept to some of the finest cooks of the twentieth century. I was particularly impressed at the generosity in time and effort of the cartoonists both of 'Fleet Street' and the Royal Academy, and would like to thank them and the other contributors most sincerely.

I am indebted to Natalie Goldsmith of the Elstree committee for all her help and advice, and to my children James, Laura and Sebastian and their friend Ellie O'Shea who helped lick stamps, address envelopes and answer the phone, then forgot who it was that called. Bless them!

Anna Hunter

Starters

WATERCRESS SOUP

HRH The Princess of Wales

1oz (25g) butter
1oz (25g) flour
1 pint (600ml) chicken stock
2 bunches, about 6oz (175g), fresh
    watercress
½ pint (300ml) single cream

Melt the butter, add flour and cook for a couple of minutes on a low heat, stirring gently. Slowly add warmed chicken stock until you have a creamy consistency. Wash the watercress thoroughly and add to the mixture. Cook slowly until the stalks are soft, stirring occasionally. This will take about 20 minutes. Remove from heat and allow to cool. Liquidize the soup and pass through a fine sieve. Chill and add the cream. Reserve a little of the cream to garnish the top of each portion. A few leaves of watercresss, previously blanched, can add additional garnish if wanted.
Serves 3

NO-COOK COLD TOMATO SOUP

Dinah Sheridan
Actress

1lb (450g) tomatoes
2tbsp chopped onion
½tsp chopped fresh tarragon (or
   ¼tsp if dried)
1tsp tomato paste (or a little more if
   using tomato ketchup)
1tsp sugar
Salt and pepper
½×5oz (½×150ml) carton soured
   cream or yogurt
Chopped chives or parsley

Wash and quarter the tomatoes and whisk
in a blender with onion and tarragon until
smooth. Rub through a sieve. Stir in the
tomato paste thoroughly with the sugar. Salt
and pepper to taste. Chill. To serve, put
a dollop of the cream or yogurt into each
bowl and swirl around. Scatter with chives or
parsley.
Serves 2

LEEK AND POTATO SOUP

Cliff Richard
Singer

1lb (450g) potatoes
2 onions
½lb (225g) leeks
2oz (50g) butter
2 pints (1 litre) chicken stock
Mixed herbs
¼ pint (150ml) natural yogurt

Peel potatoes and cut into small chunks.
Chop onions roughly. Cut leeks into
segments. Melt the butter in a large pan
and sauté the potatoes and onions for a few
minutes. Add the stock, herbs and leeks.
Simmer until potatoes are cooked. Allow to
cool for ten minutes. Mix in the yogurt, then
put the soup through a blender at maximum
speed.
   Serve hot or cold.
Serves 6

TIPS: Buy vegetables fresh and use within 48
hours. Stale vegetables should not be necessary
these days, and don't taste nearly so good.

DISLIKES: Peppers – red or green.

GARLIC SOUP

Jack Gold
Film director

6 large cloves garlic, chopped
14oz (400g) tin chopped tomatoes
2 pints (1 litre) boiling water
¼ white cabbage, thinly sliced
Salt and pepper to taste, or chicken
　cubes
Bay leaf
Handful of pasta if liked
Oil

Fry the garlic in a little oil. Add tomatoes;
bring to boil. Add boiling water, white
cabbage, seasoning, bay leaf and pasta.
Simmer for 20 minutes.
　This soup is better reheated, when all the
flavours will be released.
Serves 4

CARROT SOUP

Victoria Wood
Songwriter and comedienne

Onion
Butter
Carrots
Water
Vecon
Cream
Parsley

Sauté an onion in a lump of butter. Add a
lot of sliced carrots. Cover with boiling water
and a lump of Vecon (or a natural vegetable
stock cube). Half put the lid on and go and do
something else for a bit. Come back – blend
it, put a bit of cream in and sprinkle parsley
on top. Swallow small pieces of grit because
you never washed the parsley.
　The more you make, the more it serves.

TIPS: Plastic utensils are very difficult to clean
off cookers once they have melted.

CULINARY DISASTERS: I've had a few, but
those people have died now.

ARTICHOKE SOUP

BBC Television's *Blue Peter*

1lb (450g) Jerusalem artichokes, peeled and chopped
Small onion, peeled and chopped
½oz (15g) polyunsaturated margarine
1 pint (600ml) water or vegetable stock (if you are not a vegetarian, chicken stock may be used)
½ pint (300ml) milk
Dash of single cream (optional)
Freshly ground black pepper
Freshly ground nutmeg
Chopped parsley, chives or chopped spring onion stalks

Wash the artichokes thoroughly. Peel and cut into small even pieces. Be quite ruthless about cutting off the little lumps! Put the prepared artichokes in a bowl of cold water before you use them, so they'll keep their nice white colour.

Put the margarine into a saucepan, add the chopped onion and cook on a gentle heat for about 5 minutes. The onion should be soft but not browned otherwise you'll spoil the creamy white colour of the soup. Add the peeled and chopped artichokes to the saucepan and pour on the stock. Bring to the boil. Turn down the heat, cover and simmer for approximately 30 to 40 minutes, or until the artichokes feel soft. Remove from the heat.

Mash the mixture through a sieve to get rid of the lumps, or give a quick whirl in a liquidizer. Pour back into the saucepan and then add the milk. For a touch of luxury you can add a dash of single cream. Season with salt and freshly ground black pepper and some freshly ground nutmeg. (A pinch of powdered nutmeg if fresh is not available.) Reheat and pour into serving bowls. Garnish with some fresh chopped parsley, chives or even some tiny bits of chopped spring onion stalk.

Artichoke soup is delicious served with fresh crusty bread!

Note: If you don't have any artichokes, you could try using another root vegetable instead.
Serves 4

"WE NEVER SAY PRAYERS BEFORE MEALS! MUM'S A GOOD COOK!"

CHILLED AVOCADO SOUP

Richard O'Sullivan
Actor

1 avocado pear
1 clove garlic, crushed
1tbsp lemon juice
Chicken stock cube
½ pint (300ml) hot water
½×5oz (½×150ml) carton of yogurt
  or cream
Salt and pepper

Cut the avocado open and spoon out all the flesh. Put in the liquidizer with the crushed clove of garlic, lemon juice, chicken stock and yogurt (or cream). Add salt and freshly ground pepper and let it whirl around for about fifteen seconds. Leave it in the fridge for a couple of hours before serving.
Serves 1–2

SALMON MOUSSE

Roy Kinnear
Actor

Ask someone to buy:
2×7½oz (2×220g) tins of salmon
1 lemon
1oz (25g) packet gelatine
½ pint (300ml) double cream
Salt and pepper

Get them to:
  Take black bits off salmon. Blend salmon, grated lemon peel and juice with dissolved gelatine and double cream, and allow to set.
  After all the hard work is over, sit back and enjoy.
Serves 4

TIPS: A quick, tasty snack for summer or winter, especially for breakfast: half an avocado sprinkled with sugar and lemon.

TIPS: Try pouring French dressing instead of a knob of butter over hot, freshly cooked vegetables. It does wonders for the flavour.

TOMATO AND ORANGE SOUP

Barbara Windsor
Actress

Chicken bones
2 pints (1 litre) water
Salt
2lb (1kg) tomatoes (Use large ripe tomatoes when they are at their best. At other times use a large can of Italian tomatoes for the best flavour.)
1 onion, sliced
1 carrot, sliced
1 strip lemon rind
1 bay leaf
6 peppercorns
2oz (50g) butter
3–4tbsp plain flour
Rind and juice of ½ orange
Pepper and sugar to taste
¼ pint (150ml) single cream

To make the stock, put chicken bones into a pan with the water and a good pinch of salt. Bring the stock to the boil and reduce by a quarter by simmering.

Wipe the tomatoes and cut in half, squeezing to remove the seeds. Put tomatoes, onion and carrot into a pan with lemon rind, bay leaf, peppercorns and a good pinch of salt. Add stock to tomato mixture, put lid on and simmer until tomatoes are pulpy (about 30 minutes). Then rub through a sieve and set aside. Clean the pan, melt the butter, add the flour and make a roux. Cook out to a sandy texture. Add the tomato mixture, blend and boil. Shred the orange rind, blanch and refresh, then set aside. Add the orange juice to the soup, plus sugar and seasoning to taste. Stir in the cream at the last moment and finally add the orange peel on top. Serve at once.
Serves 6

TIPS: Marry a chef. I did!

1, 2, 3, 4, 5 PÂTÉ

Rabbi Lionel Blue
Teacher, writer, broadcaster and cook

In a processor blend together the following:
1 small onion
2 peeled and cored dessert apples
3 slices of bread without their crusts, dipped in water and squeezed dry
4 pickled herring fillets (no juice or onion)
5 hard-boiled eggs (plus 2 more to sprinkle on top)

Add 1tbsp salad oil
1tsp sugar
¼tsp white pepper
Salt to taste

Blend in batches. Mix and cover the pâté's grey appearance (it looks like a chinchilla but with a nicer taste) with the chipped yellow and white of two extra hard-boiled eggs.
Serves 4–6

TIPS: Roast pumpkin with the joint instead of roast potatoes.
LIKES: Eating the leftovers with a radio on when everyone else has gone.
DISLIKES: Soufflés and difficult dishes that make me nervous.
CULINARY DISASTERS: We bought a loaf of bread in Holland, put marmalade on it and found there was an eel baked inside it! A delicacy apparently to some. I did not taste it, so cannot comment on this aspect.

SCRAMBLED EGGS EROTIQUES AUX TOMATOES

Hardy Amies
Fashion designer

Ideal for 'souper intime'.
2 slices fried brown bread
2 ripe tomatoes
5 fresh eggs
1tbsp cream
Butter
Pepper and salt

Prepare and keep warm two slices of fried brown bread.

Skin and crush two ripe tomatoes. Season with pepper and salt. Beat lightly four fresh eggs. Melt lump of butter in small, preferably iron, saucepan, adding pepper and salt. Cook eggs, continually stirring, until they begin to coagulate. Add the tomatoes, stirring all the time. When tomatoes are hot, not necessarily cooked, add a fifth, lightly beaten, egg – stir well. Add tablespoon of cream. Serve when all is hot but not further cooked. The flavour of the new fresh egg is the secret. Pour over the fried bread. The eggs should pour, but remain on the bread.

Serve with champagne and ardour.
Serves 2

TIPS: Base every menu on what is in season.

LIKES: Enjoying dishes requested by me and cooked by my cook.

DISLIKES: All trimmings with capers in them, over-boiled potatoes, over-roasted lamb.

19

MUSHROOMS IN GARLIC BUTTER

Rt Hon Edward Heath, MP

16 good-sized open mushrooms
2 large cloves garlic, crushed
6oz (175g) soft butter
2tbsp fresh chopped parsley
1tbsp lemon juice (optional)
Salt and freshly milled black pepper

Pre-heat oven to gas mark 7, 425°F (220°C).
Wipe the mushrooms and remove stalks.
Mix the crushed garlic with the butter; add
the parsley and lemon juice and stir it well.
Season to taste. Place the mushrooms, skin
side down, in the oven-proof dish and put a
little of the garlic butter into each mushroom.
Put the dish on top shelf and let them cook
for about 10 minutes, or until the butter
is sizzling hot. Serve at once with crusty
French bread.
    Can be cooked and served in individual
dishes.
Serves 4

GRILLED SPICED GRAPEFRUIT

Countess Mountbatten of Burma

2 grapefruits
4tsp sherry
4tsp honey
Mixed spice

Cut grapefruits in half, loosen segments with
grapefruit knife, place 1tsp sherry over each
half. Repeat with 1tsp honey and sprinkle
liberally with mixed spice. Cook under the
grill (moderately hot) until grapefruit is
slightly risen and dark on the crust.
Serves 4

GRILLED GOAT'S CHEESE SALAD

Prue Leith
Cookery writer and restaurateur

8 thick slices from any fat cylindrical
    soft goat's cheese
1–2 red lettuces (radicchio)
2–3 heads Belgian chicory
3–4 red apples
1tbsp lemon juice
3oz (75g) walnut halves

For the dressing:
3tbsp salad oil
1tbsp walnut oil
2tsp vinegar
Salt and black pepper

Lay the slices of cheese in the bottom of the grill tray. Arrange radicchio and chicory leaves on eight plates, like the petals of a large flower – chicory and radicchio alternating. Using a melon baller, scoop 30 or 40 balls out of the *unskinned* apples (or cut small dice). Toss them in the lemon juice and divide them between the salads. Leave a space in the middle of each plate for the cheese. Dot the walnuts about, cover the plates and keep them in a cool place.

Shortly before dinner, whisk together the dressing ingredients and sprinkle over the salads. Just before serving, grill the cheese under blazing heat to brown the top and warm through. Lift carefully on to the salads and serve at once.
Serves 8

TIPS: Easiest way to skim fat off gravy or sauce: lay sheets of absorbent kitchen paper on the surface, lift and discard. The fat clings to the paper, the liquid runs off.

LIKES: Cooking pays my wages.

DISLIKES: Radish roses and tomato waterlilies. God made a fair job of both and they don't need improvement.

CULINARY DISASTERS: I once dropped a box containing all the knives and forks for a supper party on a Thames barge into the river at Westminster Pier. No time for replacements so my good-tempered customers ate their salmon with teaspoons as they sailed up the river.

ANGELS ON HORSEBACK

Michael Aspel
Broadcaster

8 oysters
8 rashers very finely sliced bacon
4 slices toast, without crusts

Wrap each oyster in strip of bacon and skewer with cocktail stick. Grill until bacon is crisp. Remove skewers and serve two per person, on toast.

It's a favourite of mine, because my wife doesn't like oysters, so I get more.
Serves 4

SPICY TUNA

The Hon Mrs Michael Sieff
Founder of the Michael Sieff Foundation (for the prevention of child abuse)

2×7oz (2×200g) tins tuna, drained
½ pint (300ml) mayonnaise
Worcester sauce
Cayenne pepper
Salt and pepper } **to taste**
Tomato purée
Tabasco sauce
1lb (450g) prawns
½ pint (300ml) double cream, stiffly whipped
½oz (15g) gelatine, dissolved in 3tbsp water

Flake tuna fish. Flavour mayonnaise with all the seasonings. Fold in tuna fish, prawns and cream. Stir in dissolved gelatine. Turn into 2 pint (2 litre) mould. Leave to set. Turn out and decorate. Serve with Marks & Spencer's Sour Cream and Chive dressing.
Serves 6–8

TIPS: A cleaned avocado stone can be used to give your skin a natural massage.

STUFFED TOMATO

Bob Monkhouse
Comedian and TV quiz master

Here's a recipe for a delicious and non-fattening starter!
1 beef tomato
Crab meat, fresh or tinned
Celery
Low calorie mayonnaise
Curry powder
Salt and pepper

Top the tomato and take out the seeds and excess flesh. Mix crab meat with finely chopped celery, mayonnaise and seasonings. Stuff tomato with crab meat mixture, chill and eat.
Serves 1

KIPPER PÂTÉ

Liza Goddard
Actress

1 kipper
2 hard-boiled eggs
1tbsp Hellmann's Mayonnaise
Pepper to taste

Simply blend all the ingredients and spoon into a small container, then place overnight in fridge. It's my favourite starter.
Serves 4

Peter Clayton

"Okay I give up, what was it?"

MOZZARELLA MELODY

Jeff Wayne
Composer and record producer

8oz (225g) mozzarella cheese
2 large onions
4 beef tomatoes
4tbsp oil
4tbsp vinegar
Fresh basil
Black olives
Ground pepper

Slice cheese, onions and tomatoes into thin slices. Divide into four portions. Mix oil and vinegar together (to taste) and add chopped basil. Pour oil/vinegar and basil over onions, tomatoes and cheese. Decorate with black olives. Add ground pepper to taste before serving.
    Serve with garlic bread and wine of choice.
Serves 4

CRUNCHY FISH STARTER

The Hon David Sieff
Director of Marks & Spencer

1 large apple
2 avocados
2 sticks celery   } chopped
½ cucumber
¼lb (100g) walnuts
½lb (225g) prawns
Lemon juice
Vinaigrette dressing
3tbsp mayonnaise
10 tomatoes, halved and de-seeded
8 hard-boiled eggs, halved
1 tin of tuna

Sprinkle apple and avocado with lemon juice. Mix first six ingredients together with a little vinaigrette dressing and then add most of the mayonnaise.
    Serve with Stuffed Tomatoes and Eggs:
    Stuff the tomato shells and egg whites with tuna fish mixed with a little mayonnaise and the yolk of the eggs.
    Pile all ingredients except tomatoes and eggs into centre of large flat dish and surround with tomatoes and eggs alternately.
Serves 8

DISLIKES: Complicated and fussy recipes and when it says 'Take a double saucepan . . .' or 'Line the soufflé dish with greaseproof paper . . .'!

ESCALIVADA

Claudia Roden
Cookery writer

This refreshing Spanish salad makes a good first course.

10oz (300g) medium onions
10oz (300g) green peppers
10oz (300g) red peppers
10oz (300g) aubergines
5tbsp olive oil
Salt

Put all the vegetables in a gas mark 4, 350°F (180°C) oven and leave them for between 1–2 hours, until they are very soft and the skins are brown. Put the peppers in a polythene bag and close it tight for 10 minutes to loosen their skins and make them easy to peel. When the vegetables are cool enough to handle, peel them and cut them into long thin strips. Dress simply with olive oil and a little salt. Serve them cold.
Serves 6

CHEESE APPETISER

Joanna Lumley
Actress

My favourite starters are almost always very simple. Here is a delicious cheese appetiser.

Cheddar cheese
Flour
Egg, beaten
Breadcrumbs
Oil

Chop the cheese into 1in (2cm) squares, dip into flour, then beaten egg, then breadcrumbs. Fry for about 1 minute in hot vegetable oil so that they're crisp and brown on the outside. Leave till they're cool enough to eat. Serve with pickled onions and a dry white wine.

TIPS: Keep wetting your knife under the cold tap when chopping onions – it stops the tears.

Fish & Shellfish

TROUT WITH ALMONDS

Anita Dobson
Actress

1oz (25g) plain flour
Salt
Freshly ground pepper
4 large trout, cleaned
2oz (50g) butter
2oz (50g) blanched almonds, flaked
2tsp lemon juice
Garnish
Lemon wedges
Parsley sprigs

Mix the flour with salt and pepper. Use to coat the trout. Melt the butter in a frying pan. Add the trout and brown quickly on both sides. Reduce the heat and continue cooking until the trout are tender. Transfer the fish to a warm serving dish and keep hot. Add the almonds to the pan and cook until they are golden. Stir in the lemon juice and heat through. Pour the almonds and liquid over the fish and garnish with the lemon wedges and parsley sprigs. Serve hot.
Serves 4

TANDOORI FISH

Phil Cool
Impressionist

Trout or mackerel (1 per person if main course, 1 between two if starter)
Tandoori paste
Yogurt (optional, to mix with tandoori paste)

Clean fish and pat dry with a paper towel after washing. Make diagonal cuts on both sides of the fish and cover with tandoori paste, making sure it penetrates the cuts. Leave fish to marinade for a minimum of 30 minutes. Heat the grill or barbecue and cook both sides of the fish until tender.
Serve with lemon, salad and minty yogurt.

TIPS: When filleting fish for a really fussy person, you can make sure you get every bone out by using eyebrow tweezers. But remember to wash them well before returning them to your make-up bag!

Nicola Jennings

SHAKY'S SPECIAL

Shakin' Stevens
Singer

1lb (450g) haddock fillet
½ pint (300ml) milk and 6tbsp milk
1 bay leaf
6 peppercorns
1 onion, skinned and sliced
Salt and pepper
2oz (65g) butter
3tbsp flour
2 eggs, hard-boiled and roughly
  chopped
5fl oz (150ml) single cream
2tbsp chopped fresh parsley
4oz (100g) cooked prawns
2lb (900g) potatoes, peeled
1 egg (beaten), to glaze

Place the haddock in a pan and pour over ½ pint (300ml) of milk. Add the bay leaf, peppercorns, onion and a pinch of salt. Bring to the boil and simmer for 10 minutes. Take out of pan and remove the skin and bones. Strain the liquid and keep in reserve.

Melt 1oz (40g) of the butter and stir in the flour and cook for 1 minute, stirring all the time. Remove pan from heat and gradually add the liquid in reserve. Bring to the boil and cook until thickened – 2–3 minutes. Add the eggs to the sauce with the cream, parsley, prawns and haddock. Season to taste. Put into a 2-pint (1 litre) pie dish.

Meanwhile, boil the potatoes and mash them without any liquid. Heat up the 6tbsp of milk plus the 1oz (25g) of butter left. Beat into potatoes. Either put them into a pipe bag and pipe mixture across the top, or spread it over and rough up with a fork. Bake in oven at gas mark 6, 400°F (200°C) for 10–15 minutes until the potatoes have set. Brush the beaten egg over the pie. Return to the oven for a further 15 minutes until golden brown.
Serves 4

TIPS: Make sure you have all the ingredients before you start.

CULINARY DISASTERS: None – but I'm working on it.

SMOKED HADDOCK AND AVOCADO AU GRATIN

The Duke of Westminster
Chairman of the NSPCC's
Centenary Committee

1lb (450g) smoked haddock fillet
1 pint (600ml) milk
2oz (50g) butter
2oz (50g) flour
3oz (75g) grated mature cheese
2 medium avocados, peeled and sliced
Parmesan cheese

Poach the fish in milk. When cooked, drain
and reserve the cooking liquid, putting the
fish to one side. Using extra milk if
necessary, whisk up the butter, flour and
cooking liquid to make 1¼ pints (750ml) of
sauce. Add 2oz (50g) of the grated cheese to
the sauce. Mix the cooked fish with ¾ pint
(450ml) of the cheese sauce. Put the fish
mixture into an oven-proof dish and lay slices
of peeled avocado across the top. Cover with
the remaining cheese sauce and sprinkle with
remaining grated cheese and a few shakes
of Parmesan cheese (this will aid browning).
Place in a hot oven gas mark 7, 425°F (220°C)
until golden brown and bubbling around the
edges.
Serves 3–4

PRAWN STIR-FRY

Julian Lloyd Webber
Cellist

Butter
Oil
3 courgettes, sliced
1 large onion, sliced
1 red or green pepper, sliced
6oz (175g) French beans
8oz (225g) prawns
Dry white wine
Worcester sauce
Beansprouts

Heat a little butter with a bit of oil. When
the oil is hot, add courgettes, onion, pepper
and French beans. Stir-fry the ingredients.
Next add the prawns and a dash of wine and
Worcester sauce. Finally add beansprouts
and stir-fry for a further 2 minutes.
Serves 2

TIPS: Never follow cook-book recipes exactly.
Adapt for personal preference.
LIKES: Interfering with other people's cooking.
DISLIKES: Dirty kitchens.
CULINARY DISASTERS: Chicken pie
incident. Pie placed in electric oven and oven
switched on. Unfortunately main current off so
one hour later pie completely uncooked. Problem
located – current restored. Unfortunately grill had
been set rather than oven: 15 minutes later plates
exploded – pie remained uncooked.

KEDGEREE

Felicity Kendal
Actress

Excellent for starter or main course, and is OK kept in the fridge for days.

2lb (900g) smoked haddock
2 cups rice
2tbsp garam masala
4oz (100g) butter
2 bay leaves
Black pepper

Boil the smoked haddock for about 20 minutes, remove from water, bone and flake. Boil the rice until cooked – about 15 minutes. Pour off any excess water and add the haddock, garam masala, bay leaves and some black pepper. Stir in the butter and reheat slowly.
Serves 4

QUICK KEDGEREE

Dr Alan Gilmour
Director of the NSPCC

1lb (450g) smoked haddock
4oz (100g) long grain rice
2oz (50g) butter or margarine
1 or 2 hard-boiled eggs
Parsley (or watercress) to garnish

Poach the fish. Cook the rice in boiling water. Flake the cooked fish, removing skin and bones. Drain rice, and return to pan with the flaked fish and butter, and combine the ingredients gently with a fork over a low heat. Chop the egg(s) and fold into the kedgeree. Boiled peas make a good vegetable for a light supper, and brown bread and butter to accompany.
Serves 3–4

PASTEIS
(from Portugal)

Helen Cherry
Actress

This dish should really be made with *bacalhau* – salt cod – but I find it works equally well with fresh or frozen. It's a good idea to have a hot dish in the oven so you can put the pieces in it as they are cooked.

10oz (275g) cod
10oz (275g) potatoes
1 egg
Salt, pepper and nutmeg
Parsley
Garlic, crushed

Boil the cod and remove skin and bones. Cook the potatoes and mash smoothly. Mix cod and potatoes together in ample bowl. Add chopped parsley, crushed garlic and seasoning. Add whole egg and mix well. Heat oil in a pan with a basket. Shape the mixture with two tablespoons into smooth, egg-shaped pieces, and drop into hot fat till golden brown.
   Serve with salad, and sauce tartare.
Serves 2–3

SMOKED HADDOCK
CASSEROLE

Derek Jacobi
Actor

4tbsp butter
1 medium onion, sliced
4tsp flour
2 cups milk
½ cup of grated tasty cheese
1 cup cooked rice
8oz (225g) smoked haddock, cooked
Salt and pepper
Breadcrumbs

Melt butter, fry onion until soft, add flour and milk blended together. Boil 2–3 minutes, stirring continuously. Stir in cheese, rice, haddock and seasonings. Put in greased casserole, sprinkle with breadcrumbs and dot with butter. Cook in a moderate oven gas mark 5, 375°F (190°C) for 30 minutes.
Serves 2–3

TIPS: Always use wooden chopping boards – your knives won't get blunted so quickly.

FLAKY NOODLES

Rosalie Habgood
Wife of Dr John Habgood,
Archbishop of York

½ packet shell noodles
7oz (210g) tin tuna fish
Tin of Campbell's Mushroom Soup
¼ **cup water (to moisten sauce)**
Cornflakes
Butter

Boil noodles, drain, rinse in cold water, drain again. Put in buttered oven dish. Flake tuna fish and spread over. Mix soup and water and pour over. Put cornflakes in basin with a little melted butter and stir to coat them. Spread cornflakes on top of noodle dish. Heat in oven gas mark 3, 325°F (160°C) for about ½ hour. Flakes should be brown and crisp.
Serves 3–4

Tony Husband

CULINARY DISASTERS: I made a gorgeous chocolate cake for my husband when we were just married. He thought it tasted delicious but I didn't like it and couldn't understand what was wrong with it, until a few days later when I looked for my tin of Bisto to make the gravy. There was a tin of cocoa but no Bisto!

33

PAELLA

Richard O'Sullivan
Actor

Paella is a great show-off dish. If you serve this, remember to wear the enormous sombrero you had on coming down the aircraft steps at Gatwick, back from the sunny Costa Brava!

1 chicken
Olive oil
1 large onion, sliced
1 clove garlic, chopped
12oz (350g) long grain rice
Saffron, powdered
Chicken stock cube
1 pint (600ml) water
2 large tomatoes
2 green or red peppers, sliced
½ pint (300ml) mussels
White wine
2oz (50g) garlic sausage
2oz (50g) scampi or prawns
Parsley
Lemon wedges

Get a large frying pan, joint the chicken and fry in oil until golden brown. Remove and fry the onion and garlic until soft. Add the rice and a generous pinch of saffron to the pan and keep stirring for a few minutes. Put the chicken joints back in the pan and add a pint of chicken stock made from a stock cube to cover the lot. Simmer away with a lid on the pan. Add the tomatoes and the peppers to the pan.

In another pan, cook the mussels in white wine for about 10 minutes. Pour the mussel juice into the frying pan. When the rice is just tender, chop the garlic sausage and add with the mussels and prawns. Garnish with parsley and slices of lemon and serve with a salad.
Serves 8

Reg Smythe

RICE AND TUNA FISH AU GRATIN

Penelope Keith
Actress

1 onion
Oil
8oz (225g) rice
1¾ pints (1 litre) water
7oz (210g) tin tuna fish
2oz (50g) butter
2oz (50g) flour
¾ pint (450ml) milk
8oz (225g) grated cheese
Salt and pepper
Paprika
Cayenne
Breadcrumbs

Peel and chop the onion and fry in a small amount of oil in a saucepan until tender. Add the rice and cook, stirring for another minute. Add about 1¾ pints (1 litre) of water and cook the rice, covered, for about 15 minutes or until liquid is absorbed and rice is tender.

Add the tuna fish, mix together and place in baking dish. Melt the butter in saucepan, add the flour, stir to amalgamate, and gradually add the milk. When all the milk is used and the sauce is smooth, beat in the grated cheese. When this has melted, season to taste with salt, pepper, paprika and cayenne. Remove from heat and pour over rice and fish. Sprinkle the top with breadcrumbs. Place under a hot grill and leave till top has browned, or put in hot oven gas mark 7, 425°F (220°C) for about quarter of an hour.

Serves 2

TIPS: A balloon whisk is an indispensable piece of kitchen equipment. As well as whisking eggs and cream, it will get lumps out of sauces, soups etc.

TUNA BAKE

Anthony Hopkins
Actor

8oz (225g) noodles (preferably green
  noodles)
1 large tin of tuna (packed in brine, not
  oil)
2tbsp chopped onions (can be omitted)
2 cans mushroom soup
2 small cartons of sour cream (or 1
  large, if you can find it, about
  8–10fl oz [250–300ml] required)
½ cup vermouth (can be omitted)
2tsp curry powder
1tbsp Worcester sauce
Salt and paprika to taste
Grated Cheddar cheese – about 3oz
  (75g)

Cook noodles. Drain tuna. Mix together all
the ingredients, except the Cheddar cheese,
and put into casserole. Sprinkle the cheese
over the top. Bake in oven for 30 minutes at
gas mark 4, 350°F (180°C). Can't really spoil
if left longer.
  Serve with a green salad.
Serves 4

OYSTERS WITH PÂTÉ DE FOIE GRAS

Auberon Waugh
Writer and literary critic

Not so much a recipe – more a mouth-
watering recollection of a dish eaten at the
Hôtel de France, Auch, where Monsieur
Daguin reigns.

Oysters
Butter
Pâté de foie gras
Black pepper

Heat up the grill well first. Under the grill
lay some juicy oysters, with a small knob of
butter in each shell. On each oyster arrange
a thin slice of pâté de foie gras. Sprinkle with
black pepper. Grill quickly for about a minute.
  Trumpets optional.

DISLIKES: Cabbage stalks. Roast parsnips.
Gristle in stew.

CREAMED SEAFOOD BAKE

Jeffrey Archer
Writer

For the rice:
**Long grain brown rice, measured to
10fl oz (300ml) in a glass measuring
jug**
1 pint (600ml) boiling water
½ onion, finely chopped
1tsp oil
3oz (75g) raisins

Seafood sauce:
4oz (100g) butter
4oz (100g) mushrooms, sliced
**1½lb (675g) mixed seafood, such as
prawns, halibut and scallops – sliced
or chunks**
3fl oz (75ml) dry sherry
1oz (25g) plain flour
**2tsp fresh root ginger, peeled and
grated**
2tsp hot curry powder
½tsp mustard powder
½ pint (300ml) single cream
Salt and black pepper
4oz (100g) Cheddar cheese, grated
Pinch of cayenne pepper

Set oven to gas mark 6, 400°F (200°C).
Lightly fry rice and onion in the oil for 5
minutes and add raisins. Pour on water, bring
to the boil, simmer for 40 minutes until rice is
tender.

Meanwhile, melt 2oz (50g) of the butter,
fry the mushrooms for 2–3 minutes, remove
from pan, put to one side, add another 1oz
(25g) of butter to the pan and then add
halibut, scallops and sherry. Cook for 4–5
minutes and add mushrooms. Pour remaining
butter in the pan into a jug and add last ounce
of butter back to the pan. Add flour, ginger,
curry powder and mustard and gradually stir
in the reserve fish juices and cream; season
to taste, stir and cook until thickened. Pour
this sauce over fish and mushrooms.

Arrange the rice in the base of a baking
dish 8in×12in (20cm×30cm). Spoon the fish
mixture over, sprinkle with cheese and a
dusting of cayenne pepper and bake for 30
minutes at gas mark 4, 350°F (180°C).
Serves 4–6

CULINARY DISASTERS: My wife left me to
make lunch for the two children, one aged 7 and
the other aged 5, and I decided to make them fish
and chips at their request. The special frying pan
full of oil for the chips caught on fire and so did the
kitchen.

I thought I could clean it up in the four hours
before Mary returned, but to my horror, I had
hardly begun when she set her eyes on it. She
was quite annoyed because I had to catch a plane
to America early the next morning, so not only
had the children not been fed but she had no
kitchen for about a month.

"The Mornay sauce is delicious dear, but I'm afraid the lobster is off."

Gray Joliffe

SMOKED FISH AND WATERCRESS RING

John Dankworth
Jazz musician and composer

12oz (350g) smoked fish (salmon or
   haddock)
1 onion
1 bunch watercress
½ pint (300ml) milk
2 eggs
Freshly ground black pepper
Whole prawns

Skin the fish, chop the onion and trim the
watercress. Place fish in liquidizer or food
processor with milk, onion, eggs and half
the watercress – a small amount at a time –
and blend until smooth. Add pepper to taste.
Put mixture in 1½ pint (900ml) ring mould,
cover with foil and bake in bain-marie (ie in
a dish or roasting pan half filled with water)
for 1 hour at gas mark 3, 325°F (170°C) until
firm to touch. Turn on to serving dish and
serve hot or cold, garnished with remaining
watercress and whole prawns.
Serves 2–3

CREAMY COD PIE

Dr Robert Runcie
Archbishop of Canterbury

1lb (450g) cod
1lb (450g) smoked haddock
¾ pint (450ml) milk
1½oz (40g) butter
1½oz (40g) flour
½ pint (300ml) single cream
8oz (225g) mushrooms, sliced
Chopped parsley to garnish
Mashed potato made with:
1lb (450g) potatoes
Butter and milk to bind
Salt and pepper

Bake fish in milk in a buttered fireproof dish
till cooked (about 15 minutes). Make a white
sauce with the butter, flour, milk strained off
the fish, and cream. Season. Add mushrooms
and flaked fish to the sauce. Simmer for 5
minutes, then spoon into a fireproof dish.
Cover with mashed potato and bake in oven
gas mark 4, 350°F (180°C) until potato is
golden brown (about 20 minutes). Sprinkle
with parsley.
Serves 4–6

TIPS: Roll out pastry between two layers of clear
plastic (as sold in kitchen shops). It saves a lot of
mess.

ENGLISH FISH PIE

John Mortimer
Novelist and playwright

The unwholesome and repellent food at school led me, in my schooldays, to cook omelettes according to Marcel Boulestin's instructions ('Always get the pan so hot that the almond-sized pat of butter jumps about when placed in it') over the study fire.

I think that English food, properly understood, is by far the best in the world, and I have chosen the most resolutely dull English dish in my repertoire: in fact, it's delicious.

Fish pie fills everyone up, and allows you to talk to them without a constant dash from the room to save the flaming grill or the collapsing soufflé. Cooking it has a remarkably soothing effect after a day at the Old Bailey, and many plots occur to you whilst peeling the potatoes. Cook to the accompaniment of a private bottle of Sancerre and 'The Archers'.

I have never bought a pair of scales, so it's no use asking me how much of anything.

Lots of cod or any white fish (ask the fishmonger to skin it)
Plenty of butter
Flour
Milk
7 eggs
1 small onion
Fresh parsley
2 packets of prawns (frozen will do)
1 jar mussels
Some potatoes
Salt and pepper
Grated cheese
Breadcrumbs

Grill the fish – this is important as it gives far more flavour than steaming it. Make a white sauce with the butter, flour and milk. Hardboil 6 eggs, and add them (sliced with onion and chopped parsley) to the white sauce. Add the fish when it's cooked, together with the prawns and mussels, and put the lot into a buttered, oven-proof dish. Now cream the potatoes over a low heat with a lot of butter and seasoning, break 1 egg into it and stir. Also add grated cheese to give flavour to the potatoes. Make a cover for the fish with the potatoes, and sprinkle with breadcrumbs. Cook in the oven at gas mark 4, 350°F (180°C) until golden-brown. Serve with hard white cabbage, which you should cook with a lot of butter (add a cup of water only in the last few minutes), and red cabbage cooked in brown sugar, vinegar and beer.

Open the other six bottles of Sancerre and turn off 'The Archers'.
Serves 6

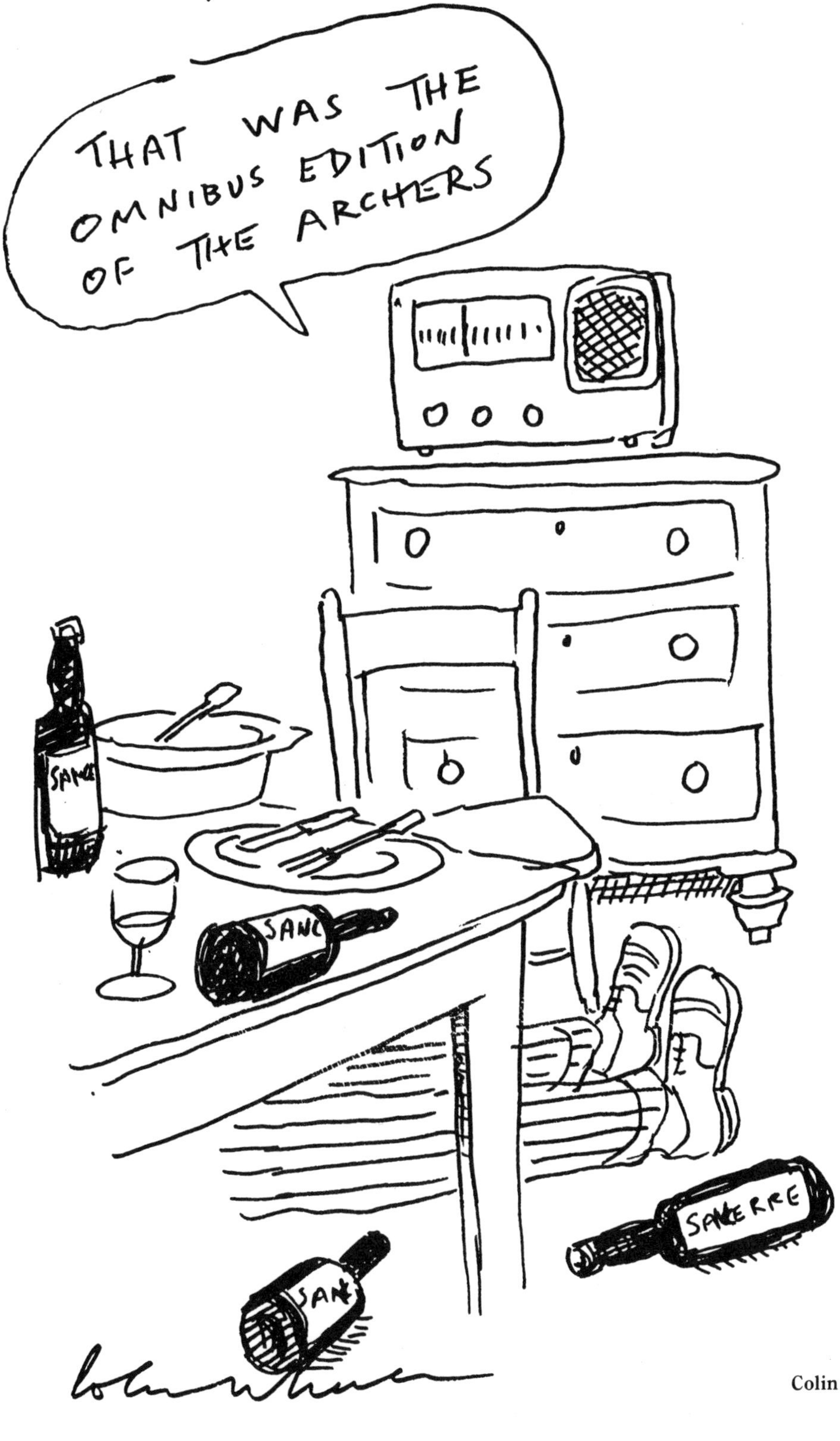

Colin Wheeler

CRAB CAKES

Jane Grigson
Cookery writer

As with any fish cakes, this Maryland recipe is best when made with freshly cooked ingredients.

1lb (500g) crab meat, or 8oz each crab and cooked skate or cod
2 slices white bread, crusts removed
1 large egg
1tsp made mustard
Dash Worcester sauce
1tbsp chopped parsley
Salt, pepper
Cayenne and paprika to taste
4 rounded tbsp mayonnaise
Clarified concentrated butter for cooking, or bacon fat

Break up the crab meat, and fish if used, with a fork so that it is flaky. Crumble the bread and mix it with the egg, mustard, Worcester sauce, parsley, seasonings and mayonnaise. Mix with the crab. Divide into six and shape with a tablespoon and knife into cakes. Fry until golden brown on both sides over a medium heat.
Note: Crab cakes are not turned in egg and breadcrumbs, like our fish cakes.
Serves 3

SCAMPI PROVENÇALE

Sir Richard Attenborough
Actor, film director and Chairman of Channel 4

1lb (450g) scampi, in seasoned flour
1oz (25g) butter, to sauté
3oz (75g) button mushrooms, sliced
3 tomatoes – skinned, hard stalk and seeds removed
5oz (150g) boiled rice

Sauce:
2 shallots, finely chopped
Bouquet garni
1 glass white wine
1oz (25g) butter
½oz (15g) flour
1 clove garlic, crushed with ½tsp salt
1tsp tomato purée
½ pint (300ml) stock

Simmer the shallots with bouquet garni and wine until liquor is reduced by half, then remove bouquet garni and set sauce aside.

In another pan, melt butter, add flour, brown lightly then add garlic, tomato purée and stock. Simmer for 10–15 minutes, then pour in reduced wine and cook for a further 5 minutes. Draw aside and add small shavings of butter. Keep hot. Roll scampi in seasoned flour and, in another pan, sauté lightly in butter for 5–6 minutes. Lift into serving dish. Sauté mushrooms in the pan and add to sauce with tomatoes, roughly chopped. Reboil for 1 minute, then spoon over scampi. Serve with rice.
Serves 4

Meat & Poultry

LIVER MOULEE

Paul Young
Singer

2 large onions, finely sliced
1/3 cup of cooking oil
3 cloves of garlic, finely chopped
1tsp dry ginger
1tsp cumin powder
1/2tsp chilli powder
1tsp turmeric powder
1/2tsp garam masala
1/3 cup water
3/4lb (350g) lamb's liver
1/3 block of creamed coconut
1tsp sugar
1/2tsp salt
1dssp lemon juice

Cook onions in oil gently until soft and slightly brown. Switch up heat to medium, add garlic. Cook for 15 seconds, add dry ginger, cumin, chilli, turmeric powder and garam masala. Stir for approximately 2 minutes, taking care not to let the ingredients stick or burn, then add 1/3 cup of water and simmer gently. Clean and chop the liver into 1/2in (1cm) thick pieces (cleaning off the membranes now means less trouble for the guests!), wash and drain. Add creamed coconut (you'll find it in most Indian-owned supermarkets) and stir, until dissolved, at medium heat. Add liver, sugar and salt. Stir for two minutes. Switch down low for 3 minutes and add lemon juice and stir. Pour into a heated dish and serve with pilao rice.
Serves 4

TIPS: Don't worry too much about measures; for some reason, as long as you add your ingredients with *flair*, it seems to taste better!

LIKES: The same as with every hobby or job, I love to see people enjoy it.

DISLIKES: I'm still trying hard to eat raw oysters; in fact, I prefer most food at least blanched but not too well done.

CULINARY DISASTERS: I recently tried to fillet a fish. *That* was a disaster!

BEEF STROGANOFF

Michael Parkinson
Broadcaster and journalist

2lb (900g) fillet steak
Seasoned flour
2 onions, chopped
3oz (75g) butter
8oz (225g) mushrooms, sliced
½ glass white wine
¼ pint (150ml) double cream
Salt and pepper

Cut the steak into strips and toss in seasoned flour to coat generously. Fry the onions in 2oz (50g) butter until transparent. Add the meat and cook quickly to seal, turning constantly. Add the remaining butter and cook the mushrooms for 2 minutes. Remove from heat. Stir in the wine and cream and reheat gently without boiling. Season to taste and serve with rice and salad.
Serves 4

LASAGNE CASSEROLE

Dorothy Tutin
Actress

1lb (450g) minced beef, crumbled
2 cloves garlic, crushed
2tbsp salad oil
8oz (225g) tin tomato sauce
Large tin tomatoes
1tsp salt
¼tsp pepper
½tsp marjoram
8oz (225g) noodles, cooked
8oz (225g) thinly sliced Cheddar
    cheese
12oz (350g) cottage cheese
½ cup grated Parmesan

Sauté the minced beef and garlic in the oil, then add the next five items and simmer for 20 minutes. While it simmers, cook those noodles in boiling salted water for about 15 minutes, and drain them. Now fill a big buttered casserole with alternate layers of the noodles, cheese, tomato-meat sauce and Parmesan, ending with a layer of sauce and Parmesan. Bake it, uncovered, at gas mark 5, 375°F (190°C) for 20 minutes.

You can do this the day before, and just reheat it.
Serves 6 (Recipe by courtesy of Amanda Waring)

TIPS: Serve hot, freshly cooked spaghetti with finely ground walnuts, olive oil, salt and pepper. A deliciously simple Tuscan recipe.

KAHAB
(Sauté of Veal)

John Amis
My Music panellist and whistler

Enough for three greedy (like myself) persons, four at a pinch. Sometimes I add mushrooms or bacon, even both – then it's enough for four to five (and it's good the next day, heated up).

1lb (450g) fillet or neck of veal
2oz (50g) butter
Salt and pepper
¼tsp caraway seeds
1 very small onion, thinly sliced
½ lemon, thinly sliced
½ pint (300ml) sour cream
For garnishing: slices of lemon and
    tufts of parsley

Cut the meat free from skin and bone into pieces about 2in (5cm) square and about ½in (1.5cm) in thickness. Heat the butter in a fireproof earthenware cooking pot, put in the meat, season to taste with salt and pepper, add the caraway seeds, sliced onion and lemon, and fry gently for 10 minutes. Now add the cream, cover closely and cook gently in the oven gas mark 4, 350°F (180°C) for about ¾ hour, or until tender.

Serve garnished with thin slices of lemon and sprigs of parsley.
Serves 3

DIANA'S STEW

Donald Sinden
Actor

As cooked by my wife, Diana. I wouldn't know where to begin!

4oz (100g) butter
2lb (900g) stewing steak
2lb (900g) bag of frozen petit pois
1 small chopped onion
1tbsp sugar
Salt and pepper to season

First put the butter in the bottom of a large heavy casserole. On top of it put the steak (not cut up). Add the peas, chopped onion, sugar, and the seasoning. Cover and place in a pre-heated oven gas mark ¼, 225°F (110°C) for 6 hours.

You then have a delicious casserole either for a dinner party of 4–6 people, or for a family lunch. Serve with baked potatoes in their jackets.
Serves 4–6

TIPS: Have a good take-away nearby, mine is superb – Justin de Blank in Elizabeth Street, London SW1.

DISLIKES: Tripe.

KILLER CHILLI

Lenny Henry
Comedian

You will need:

2 big onions
2 green peppers
4oz (100g) butter
1lb (450g) minced beef
Tin of Italian tomatoes
1tbsp tomato purée
Chilli powder (mild or hot dependent on
    whether your tongue is made of
    leather)
Pinch oregano
Pinch mixed spices
Pinch ground cloves
¼lb (100g) mushrooms
Tin of kidney beans
Dash tabasco
2 beef Oxo cubes
Glass of red wine
Lucky rabbit's foot

This is what you do:
Place rabbit's foot round your neck (you're going to need all the luck you can get, because I certainly don't know what I'm doing).

Chop onions and green peppers. Fry in butter until they are fairly translucent (that means see-through, Thicky). Add the meat and fry until it is brown. Add tomatoes and stir for a couple of minutes until it is bubbling noisily. Add tomato purée, and stir until sauce thickens. Add all the spices and herbs, chop mushrooms, add them, and stir for 2 minutes. Add kidney beans and give it a good stir. Add dash of tabasco and crumble in Oxo cubes and wine and stir again.

Put on a low heat – eg gas mark 2, 300°F (150°C) – and simmer for about 1 hour, stirring occasionally. After this time it should be a lovely dark brown colour and quite thick. If there is a layer of fat on top, scrape off with a spoon. Yum Yum in my tum.

Serve with rice or pitta bread to about four people.
Serves 4

"It was a misprint in the Recipe Book"

John Anscomb

STEAK AND KIDNEY PUD

Russell Grant
Astrologer

Suet Crust
8oz (225g) plain flour
4oz (100g) shredded suet
Salt
Cold water

Filling
1lb (450g) chuck steak, cubed
4oz (100g) ox kidney, cut up
Seasoned flour
Dripping (beef for preference) for frying
2 onions

Gravy
2 beef cubes
1tsp each of Worcester Sauce and
   Marmite. Make up to 1 pint (600ml)
   with hot water

To make the suet pastry, mix flour, suet and little salt and add enough cold water to make a dough. Allow to rest before rolling out.

Roll the steak and kidney in seasoned flour and gently fry in beef dripping to seal in flavour. Fry the onions for about a minute. Roll out pastry and line a 2 pint (1 litre) sized basin, leaving enough pastry to make a lid. Put in the steak, kidney and onions and pour in gravy, but not enough to fill the basin. Put on the lid and seal the edges well. Cover with greaseproof paper and kitchen foil and steam for 4 to 5 hours.

Serve with mashed spuds and cabbage.
Serves 4

LIKES: I find cooking therapeutic.

DISLIKES: Liver.

CULINARY DISASTERS: Eating far too much!

LAMB COOKED AS MELON

Janet Laurence
Cookery writer

Shoulder of lamb is superb meat and cheaper than leg. Getting rid of the awkwardly shaped bone means carving is simple and that an interesting stuffing can be added. The following recipe trusses the meat into the shape of a cantaloup melon. It looks very impressive brought to the table surrounded with spring vegetables or watercress. Cut it like a cake, thick slices are easiest.

1tbsp olive oil or butter
1 medium onion, finely chopped
1 clove garlic, peeled and finely chopped
4oz (100g) mushrooms, sliced
1 large shoulder of lamb, boned out flat
1 tin smoked oysters
1tbsp chopped parsley
1tbsp chopped mixed herbs (chervil, tarragon, rosemary if possible)
Salt and freshly ground black pepper
1 large onion, roughly chopped
4 sticks celery, roughly chopped
3 carrots, roughly chopped
2tbsp olive oil
½ pint (300ml) dry white wine
½ pint (300ml) lamb or chicken stock

Sauce:
8oz (225g) mushrooms, sliced
2tbsp olive oil or butter or mixture
1 clove garlic, finely chopped

Gently heat the oil or butter, add the onion and garlic, cook gently until onion transparent. Add sliced mushrooms, raise heat and cook until mushroom liquid is released and evaporated. Lay out the meat, skin side downwards. Season, add the drained oysters, the onion and mushroom mixture and the chopped herbs, covering the inside of the meat, and season. Bring two edges of the meat together over the stuffing and secure by sewing together with string and a trussing needle, tying the thread in a big knot. Repeat with the other sides, making a reasonably neat parcel. Then take approximately 1.5 metres (about 4½ feet) of string. Bring the middle of the string round the packet of meat, twist it and take it back again, dividing the meat into quarters; then halve each quarter, so that the packet resembles a melon-shaped ball. Finally tie string into a big bow.

Heat the two tablespoons of oil in flame-proof casserole. Brown meat on all sides. Set aside. Add the chopped vegetables and cook gently until just beginning to brown. Add wine and stock, deglaze bottom of pan and bring to boil. Place meat on top of vegetables and season. Cover casserole and place in pre-heated oven at gas mark 4, 350°F (180°C) and cook for approximately 2–2½ hours until meat ready.

Approximately 30 minutes before meat is cooked, pour off most of cooking juices. Skim fat from top of juices, then reduce slightly. Heat oil or butter, add mushrooms and cook quickly to release juices and evaporate off. Lower heat, add garlic and cook gently for 10–15 minutes until mushrooms very tender. Add reduced juices and check seasoning.

When meat is ready, remove from casserole. Remove all strings and keep meat warm. Strain rest of juices and skim off fat. Add degreased juices to sauce and check seasoning. Cut meat as you would a cake and serve with the sauce. Garnish with spring vegetables or watercress.
Serves 6–8

TIPS: Make sure you have a trussing needle before embarking on this recipe, because it's pretty well impossible to do without one. You can get them at any good kitchen equipment shop – or you could try scrounging one off your local butcher.

CHICKEN, TONGUE AND LEEK PIE

Michael Crawford
Actor and singer

1 boiling chicken
1 onion
1 bay leaf and seasoning
4 good-sized leeks (well cleaned)
4oz (100g) cooked tongue
¼ pint (150ml) double cream (gently warmed)
8oz (225g) shortcrust pastry

Boil chicken with onion, bay leaf and seasoning until tender, and leave to cool. Keep the stock.

Grease an ovenproof dish with butter. Cut cooked chicken into 1 inch (2.5cm) pieces and cut leeks into rounds. Then place one layer of chicken pieces in prepared dish, and season, then one layer of leeks. Continue placing layers of chicken and leeks alternately until ingredients are used up. Cover with a layer of cooked tongue; pour over stock from boiled chicken, leaving enough space for expansion. Cover the pie dish with shortcrust pastry. Pre-heat oven to gas mark 5, 375°F (190°C), and bake for 30 minutes. Remove from oven, make a hole in the pastry crust and pour in the warmed double cream. Replace in oven for a further 15 minutes.
Serves 4–6

HOT POT

Sir Cyril Smith, MP

1lb (450g) beef chuck steak, cut into 1in (2.5cm) pieces
3tsp salt
Fat
2fl oz (65ml) water
6 medium potatoes, peeled and sliced
4 medium onions, peeled and sliced
6 carrots, peeled and sliced
½tsp tabasco
1lb (450g) tin tomatoes

Sprinkle beef with salt, brown thoroughly in a small amount of fat. Remove beef. Add water to fat in pan. Cook, stirring constantly to blend bits of meat left in pan. Remove from heat.

Layer beef, potatoes, onions and carrots in casserole, sprinkling each layer with salt and a little tabasco, and adding tomatoes on each layer. Pour water and fat over (top layer being potato). Cook in medium oven gas mark 4, 350°F (180°C) for at least 2 hours.
Serves 4

TIPS: There's an old French tradition that says whoever receives a bay leaf in their meal has to make love to the chef (or cook). Don't say you weren't warned!

FRANKLIN

CORONATION CHICKEN

Ernie Wise
Comedian

This recipe is best if made the day before the day it is required.

½oz (15g) butter
1 medium onion, chopped
2tsp curry powder
5fl oz (¼ pint) chicken stock
1tbsp tomato purée
3tbsp mango chutney
2tbsp apricot jam
2tsp lemon juice
Salt and pepper
Paprika
8–10tbsp mayonnaise
4tbsp single cream
8 large chicken breasts cut in pieces

Melt the butter in a pan. Add the onion and cook till soft. Stir in curry powder and cook for 2 minutes. Add the chicken stock and mix well. Blend in the tomato purée, chutney and apricot jam, and simmer until thicker. Add lemon juice and seasoning, then strain and leave to cool. Gradually whisk in the mayonnaise and cream. Place chicken in large serving dish, pour sauce over and sprinkle with paprika.
Serves 8

OXTAIL

John Arlott
Cricket writer and wine expert

Carrots, sliced	Salt and pepper
Onions	Mace
Oil	Allspice
1 oxtail	1tbsp tomato paste
1 cow heel	2 garlic cloves,
Flour	crushed
Dry red wine	Bouquet garni
Beef stock	Brandy

Sauté vegetables in hot oil and place in bottom of slow crock or casserole. Dredge oxtail and cow heel in flour and brown in oil. Transfer to slow crock. Add plenty of good, dry red wine and plenty of beef stock. Flavour with pepper, salt, pinch of mace and allspice; add tomato paste mixed with red wine, the crushed garlic cloves and bouquet garni. Add generous splash of brandy. Cook for 8–10 hours in very slow oven, until the meat falls from the joints.

Before serving, remove cow heel and bouquet garni, skim off excess fat and adjust seasoning. Keep it warm and keep warm yourself.
Serves 4

CULINARY DISASTERS: The greatest of culinary disasters was, when about to slosh brandy from a very full bottle into the oxtail, rather late in the proceedings, I dropped the bottle into the brew, which was too hot for it to be pulled out by hand. Most of my drinking friends found the resultant brew too strong – but not all.

TORTILLA FLAT

Beryl Bainbridge
Writer

This is a dish made by the gypsies of Andalusia, at least that is what I was told when I was in Spain 35 years ago.

4 eggs
4lb (2.5kg) of large peeled potatoes
Bits of bacon
or
Bits of sausage
or
Bits of corned beef
2 big onions, sliced
Any old tomatoes
Any old green peppers
Oil
Garlic, salt and pepper to taste

Smash eggs in a bowl and turn the potatoes into chips, and then into cubes (about the size of a small dice). Drop pieces into the bowl and swill about. Fry meat, bacon, onion, scraps, etc, in oil and add to bowl. Pour contents of bowl into a large frying pan lined with a film of oil. Fry like mad, making sure that the mixture does not stick to the bottom. Place a large plate over frying pan and with a quick flip, turn over. This should, perhaps, be done over a clean bath in case of accidents. One side will now resemble a very tough omelette, the underside will be very mushy. Put in more oil and slide tortilla, mushy side down, into pan. Keep shaking. The result should be a bit like a sponge cake, only made of chips. Next, travel to Spain and ask any gypsy for a very large flat loaf. Bring back and place tortilla inside. It can be cut like a cake and will keep for a month in the deep freeze and 2 days hanging from the saddle of your mule. If eaten at home in the city one can still cry *olé* while munching.
Serves 8

CULINARY DISASTERS: I've had too many to list. My children were the only ones who enjoyed school dinners!

BITOKES À LA RUSSE
(Hamburgers with cream sauce)

Ronnie Corbett
Comedian

1½lb (675g) lean minced beef
3oz (75g) onion, finely chopped
1oz (25g) softened butter, ground beef
  suet or fresh pork fat
1½tsp salt
⅛tsp pepper
⅛tsp thyme
1 egg
1dssp oil and ½oz (15g) butter for
  frying

For sauce:
⅛ pint (75ml) stock or beef bouillon
¼ pint (150ml) cream
Salt and pepper
Pinch of nutmeg
Lemon juice
1–1½oz (25g–40g) softened butter
2tbsp chopped green herbs, such as
  parsley, chives, tarragon, chervil OR
  parsley only

Add beef, butter or fat, seasonings and egg to the onions in a mixing bowl, and beat vigorously to blend thoroughly. Correct seasoning. Form into patties ¾in (1.5cm) thick. Take ½oz (15g) butter and 1dssp oil, or enough to film bottom of frying pan. Cook over moderate heat. Remove to hot serving dish.

Pour the fat out of the frying pan. Add the stock or bouillon and boil it down rapidly, scraping up coagulates, cooking juices until reduced almost to a syrup. Pour in cream and boil it down rapidly for a minute or two until it has been reduced and thickened slightly. Season to taste with salt, pepper, nutmeg and drops of lemon juice.

Remove the frying pan away from the heat, swirl in the butter by dessert spoon until it is absorbed. Stir in the herbs, spoon the same over the hamburgers and serve.
Serves 4

John Burns

JERSEY BEAN CROCK

Wendy Richards
Actress

This is a traditional Channel Island dish.

2lb (900g) mixed dried beans
1 hock or 2 trotters
2lb (900g) belly pork
1 large onion
Pepper and a little salt

Soak beans overnight. Place ingredients in large pot or casserole. Add plenty of water. Place in oven gas mark 1, 275°F (140°C) for about 12 hours. Remove fat and bone from meat. Season. A little dry cider may be added.
Serves 6

SWISS STEAK

Angela Rippon
Broadcaster

4 slices topside of beef, each weighing
  about 6oz (175g)
1½oz (40g) flour
1 level tsp salt
¼tsp pepper
1½oz (40g) lard
2 onions, finely sliced
2 sticks celery, chopped
8oz (225g) tin tomatoes
2 level tsp tomato purée
½tsp Worcester sauce
¼ pint (150ml) water

Cut steak into 8 pieces. Mix together flour, salt and pepper. Toss meat in flour mixture, pressing it in so that all flour is used. Melt lard in a pan and fry meat quickly on all sides until it is brown. Transfer meat to an oven-proof casserole. Add onion and celery to fat remaining in pan. Fry until pale golden brown, then add to the meat with tomatoes, tomato purée, Worcester sauce and water. Cover casserole and cook in a very moderate oven for 2½ hours, or until meat is tender. Oven setting: gas mark 2, 300°F (150°C).
Serves 4

TIPS: Don't let men in the kitchen – they turn the gas too high under the pans!

LIKES: I like creating new dishes, this mainly means pouring more wine into things.

DISLIKES: I loathe cleaning pans after scrambled eggs; this is the time to let the men into the kitchen.

CULINARY DISASTERS: A Benedictine soufflé. But it was fun scraping the dish out!

DUCK À L'ORANGE

Helen Cherry
Actress

4–5lb (2–2½kg) fresh duckling
3 oranges
1oz (25g) butter
Salt and black pepper
1 rounded tbsp granulated sugar
1tsp runny honey
⅓ pint (200ml) chicken stock
1tbsp lemon juice
2tbsp brandy

Insert three slices of orange into the cavity, and place duck on a rack in a roasting tin. Put giblets under or round the rack. Smear the breast with butter, salt and pepper and roast in a pre-heated moderate oven gas mark 4, 350°F (180°C).

Allow 20–25 minutes per lb (½kg). While the duck is cooking, remove the rind from one orange, cut into very thin strips, and cover with water. Boil for 5 minutes; drain. Cut skinless segments from one orange and squeeze juice from the rest. Heat the sugar and 2tbsp of water in a pan until caramelised, add chicken stock and heat gently till the caramel is dissolved.

About 15 minutes before the duck is cooked, spread a little runny honey over the breast. When cooked, the breast should be crisp and brown. Remove the duck to a platter (or serving dish) and keep warm. Skim the fat from the roasting tin, add chicken stock, orange juice, lemon juice and brandy. Stir and boil, and when reduced, strain over duck.

Garnish with orange strips and segments.
Serves 2

Annie Tempest

VROOM-VROOM CHILLI

Pamela Bell
Wife of racing driver Derek Bell

1lb (450g) cubed lean beef
Oil
1tbsp chilli powder
1tsp minced onion
Salt to taste
1 cup tomato juice
½tsp garlic powder or minced garlic
½tsp freshly ground black pepper
1 tin kidney beans

Brown the meat in oil, and drain. Add all the other ingredients (except beans). Simmer a while. Add the beans, warm up, then serve. May be topped with cheese, raw onions or a piquant sauce.
Serves 4

PORK WITH DATES

Bryan Gould, MP

This is a recipe for a dish which I often make for my own family. I find cooking a marvellous relaxation and enjoy eating the results.

1 large onion
Oil
Butter
1lb (450g) pork fillet, cubed
1tsp allspice
1tsp juniper berries
Salt and pepper
1 glass white wine
2oz (50g) chopped dates
4oz (100g) mushrooms
2fl oz (60ml) cream
1tsp cornflour

Chop and sauté onion in a little oil and butter. Add cubed pork fillet, and sauté. Add allspice and juniper berries and salt and pepper to taste. Add the wine and simmer for 15 minutes. Add chopped dates and mushrooms and simmer for a further 15 minutes. Add cream and cornflour dissolved in half a cup of water. Adjust seasoning and add more liquid if necessary.
Serves 4

TIPS: Use chopped dates instead of dried fruit in baking; they're delicious and cheaper.

SAVOURY PORK CHOPS

Russell Harty
Broadcaster and journalist

4 pork chops
4 apples
1 large onion
4 tomatoes
Salt and pepper
Butter
½ pint (300ml) cold water
1tbsp vinegar (approx)
1tbsp brown sugar (approx)

Fry chops for a few moments to seal in juices. Put in casserole, grate apples and onion over them. Cut tomatoes in slices and put on top. Season with salt and pepper. Add butter and cold water, vinegar and brown sugar mixed, to taste. Cook for 1 hour at medium heat, gas mark 4, 350°F (180°C).
Serves 4

BROWNED DEVILLED CHICKEN

Ernie Wise
Comedian

4 chicken joints, skinned or not as you like
2oz (50g) margarine
2 level tsp dry mustard
1 level tsp curry powder
1 level tsp caster sugar
1 level tbsp plain flour
1 rounded tbsp sweet brown pickle
1 tbsp Worcester sauce

Combine all the ingredients and mix well together. Spread over the chicken. Bake in a suitable container at gas mark 5, 375°F (190°C) for 1 hour.
Serves 4

TIPS: To ripen avocados quickly, put them in a brown paper bag along with a ripe banana and keep in a warm place.

STUFFED PEPPERS

George Cole
Actor

1 large onion, chopped finely
Olive oil
3 rashers streaky bacon, chopped
1dssp oregano
3–4 cloves garlic, chopped finely
1lb (450g) minced beef steak
2oz (50g) rice, cooked and drained
1tbsp tomato paste
Salt and black pepper
4 medium-sized peppers

Fry onion until tender in olive oil; add bacon, oregano and garlic. When brown, add the minced steak. Cook on a medium heat, stirring regularly for 5 minutes. Add the cooked rice, tomato paste to bind, and salt and pepper. Slice off the tops of the peppers, remove seeds and wash. Fill with the meat mixture. Place in an oven-proof dish, cover for the first 40 minutes, then remove cover for a further 20 minutes in a hot oven, gas mark 7, 425°F (220°C).
    Serve with rice and a fresh tomato sauce.
Serves 4

FAMOUS HUNT STEW

Gareth Hunt
Actor

2lb (900g) beef or lamb, cut into small
    pieces
Plain flour
Cooking oil
1lb (450g) potatoes, sliced
1lb (450g) carrots, sliced
1lb (450g) parsnips, chopped
2 onions, sliced
2tbsp barley
2tsp garlic salt
4 garlic cloves, crushed
3tsp mixed herbs
1tsp curry powder
1 pint (600ml) beef stock

Roll meat in flour and fry in oil to seal. Transfer to a large cooking pot, add all the other ingredients and pour the stock over. This stew is at its best when it has been simmering for a few hours, so cook gently at about gas mark 3, 325°F (160°C).
Serves 6

TIPS: When stir-frying, slice all the ingredients roughly the same thickness so they take the same amount of time to cook through.

SULIMAN'S PILAFF

Raymond Briggs
Author and illustrator of
children's books

I have borrowed this recipe from Elizabeth David's *A Book of Mediterranean Food*, with the author's kind permission. It is marvellously simple to do, so there's nothing to go wrong! I've never known anyone not to like it.

Dripping or cooking oil
2 cups of rice
4 pints (2 litres) boiling water
Roasted leg of lamb cut into small
   pieces
2 onions, sliced
Handful raisins
Handful currants
1 large clove garlic, crushed
6 ripe tomatoes
Handful pine nuts (or roasted almonds)
1 small carton soured cream or yogurt

Into a thick pan put 3 or 4tbsp of good dripping or oil and when it is warm put 2 cupfuls of rice and stir for a few minutes until it takes on a transparent look. Then pour over about 4 pints (2 litres) of boiling water and cook very fast for about 12 minutes. The time of cooking varies according to the rice, but it should be under- rather than over-done.

In the meanwhile have ready a savoury preparation of small pieces of cooked lamb, fried onions, raisins, currants, garlic, tomatoes and pine nuts, if you can get them, or roasted almonds – all sautéd in dripping with plenty of seasoning. Put your strained rice into a thick pan and stir in the meat and onion mixture, add a little more dripping if necessary and stir for a few minutes over a low flame before serving. Hand the pilaff round with a bowl of sour cream or yogurt.

Yum yum!
Serves 4
[Suliman was Elizabeth David's Sudanese cook in Cairo from 1941 to 1946.]

TIPS: Despite the cost, always use stainless steel saucepans. Aluminium gets into the brain.

DISLIKES: The Paris *pissoir* smell of boiling cabbage.

CULINARY DISASTERS: Grandly carving the Christmas turkey and finding the plastic bag of giblets still inside.

PASTA ALL' AMATRICIANA

James Bellini
Writer and broadcaster

Introduced to me by one Sergio Borfecchia, a Roman adventurer descended from the inventor of the roulette wheel.

Despite its utter simplicity, this tasty pasta dish, beloved of the peasants of Abruzzi, south-east of Rome, remained a well-guarded secret for centuries. Even today few Italian restaurants in Britain feature it on their menus, though a quiet word to a friendly chef can sometimes yield a steaming plateful within minutes.

12oz (300g) pasta
8 rashers bacon (panchetta, if you can get it)
2 large tins plum tomatoes
1 glass red wine
4 or 5 garlic cloves (peeled and crushed)
Splash of olive oil (cooking oil will do)
Large knob of butter
Parmesan cheese (freshly grated if possible)
OR Peccorino cheese

The Sauce:
Practically any type of pasta will work wonderfully with this sauce.

Into a hot frying pan drop penny-sized pieces of bacon. Two rashers per person should suffice. Aficionados use *panchetta*. Before the sizzling bacon begins to brown, add Neapolitan peeled plum tomatoes. Two cans will be enough for four people. Add a glass of red wine, along with four or five cloves of fresh garlic, peeled and crushed.

This mixture should then be reduced over a strong flame until most of the fluid has evaporated, leaving the sauce with the consistency of slightly watery polyfilla (another pasta sauce even more secret than Amatriciana). Leave the sauce standing for as long as possible. Sauces like this improve with age as the ingredients bind together and exchange flavours. Try making a bulk order and freeze the surplus; it'll taste even better a week later.

The Pasta:
Into boiling, salted water drop a couple of spoonfuls of olive oil. Then add the pasta of your choice. Exactly how much is a matter of individual appetites. (Cold pasta makes an excellent salad base in case you overestimate.)

After a couple of minutes test frequently by lifting out a piece with a fork and biting into it; when there is just the merest hint of hardness at the centre, pour the pasta into a collander to drain. It will dry very quickly. Drop back into the still hot, empty pan and add a couple of knobs of butter. Then add the thick sauce to the pasta, working it like a dressed salad with two metal forks to make sure the pasta is well-coated.

Serve in mildly gaudy flowered bowls bought in Vietri during your last Italian vacation. Sprinkle copiously with freshly grated parmesan, or try a soft cheese such as *peccorino* for a delightful change. A side dish of chicory and fennel smothered in lemon-enhanced vinaigrette completes the picture, alongside a bottle of bold red Italian wine. Think of Amalfi or Sorrento.
Serves 4

TIPS: When making G&Ts and V&Ts, avoid excessive dilution of gin or vodka through melting ice cubes by pouring tonic into the ice tray instead of water. Once frozen it makes a much less intrusive cooling agent.

MOUSSAKA

Nicholas Parsons
Actor

1lb (450g) aubergines, sliced
Salt and pepper
2 large onions, skinned and sliced
1 garlic clove, skinned and finely
  chopped
6tbsp vegetable oil
1½lb (775g) minced lamb
1 level tbsp flour
14oz (400g) tin tomatoes
½ pint (300ml) natural yogurt
2 eggs, beaten
½tsp grated nutmeg
1oz (25g) grated Parmesan cheese

Place the aubergine slices in a colander, sprinkling each layer with salt. Cover and leave for 30 minutes to extract the bitter juices. Meanwhile, fry the onions and garlic in 2tbsp oil for 5 minutes until golden. Add the meat and fry for a further 10 minutes until browned, then add the flour and cook for a minute. Add the tomatoes with their juice, season and simmer for 20 minutes.

Drain the aubergine slices, rinse and pat dry. Heat the remaining oil in a frying pan and fry the aubergine slices for 4–5 minutes, turning once. Add more oil if necessary. Arrange a layer of aubergines in the bottom of a large oven-proof dish and spoon over a layer of meat. Continue the layers until all the meat and aubergines are used.

Beat the yogurt, eggs, seasoning and nutmeg together and stir in half the Parmesan. Pour over the dish and sprinkle with the remaining cheese. Bake in the oven at gas mark 4, 350°F (180°C) for about 45 minutes until golden.
Serves 4

Glen Baxter

YOUNG HOWARD COULD NOT FACE ANOTHER MOUSSAKA

TIPS: Wash up as you go – or better still find someone else to do the washing up!

DISLIKES: Cream and fats make me ill, so I prefer dishes cooked in oil or wine. Unfortunately, I don't like the smell of garlic, so I could never be a chef.

CULINARY DISASTERS: When I was six my parents told me some people cooked and ate snails. Next day I collected some from the garden, and to surprise my parents tried to cook them – with disastrous results!

63

A Very High Hen.

Annie Tempest

CHICKEN WITH PEACHES

Barbara Cartland and her chef Nigel Gordon

Peaches are indigenous to Persia and were introduced into England in 1524 by Wolf, the gardener to Henry VIII who brought in apricots at the same time.

A peach is one of the best revivers known for the loss of taste and smell. It has a marked action on the membranes of the eyes, nose and mouth.

1×4lb (1×2kg) roasting chicken
1tbsp butter
2 small onions, sliced
2 medium carrots, sliced
2oz (50g) bacon rashers, chopped
14oz (400g) tin peaches
1tsp dried thyme
1 bay leaf
Salt and pepper
3 fresh peaches, peeled, stoned and cut
  in half
Watercress and parsley to garnish

Roast the chicken in a hot oven, gas mark 6, 400°F (200°C) until cooked – about 1 hour.

Meanwhile, make the sauce. Melt the butter in a saucepan, add the onions, carrots and bacon and cook slowly for about 15 minutes. Then add the peaches, thyme, bay leaf, salt and pepper, and cover to cook for a few minutes. Put the whole lot in the liquidizer for a few seconds and adjust the seasoning. Remove the chicken from the oven, carve and cover with sauce. Then garnish with the fresh peaches, watercress and parsley.
Serves 4

TIPS: Roast poultry upside down so the juices run into the breast.

SPAGHETTI ALLA CARBONARA

William Franklyn
Actor

This can be served, for full effect, on a low table on a very thick hearthrug in front of a log fire and washed down by a Villa Antinoni Chianti Classico or an Orlando Cabernet-Sauvignon '84 (Australian).

¾lb–1lb (350–450g) smoked bacon, cut thick
1 packet spaghetti
Butter
4 eggs
6–8oz (175–225g) grated Cheddar cheese, or other mild cheese
Black pepper
4tbsp double cream (optional)

Cut the bacon into strips and cook until the fat starts to become crunchy. Set aside. Cook the spaghetti in boiling water until tender with very little salt. Do not overcook. Drain spaghetti well and toss with a small knob of butter. Add the raw eggs one by one, stirring carefully over the lowest heat possible. Next stir in cheese until melted, and finally the bacon. Season with home-ground black pepper and serve immediately in hot soup plates. If desired, the double cream may be stirred in as a final boost to your cholesterol.

Serve with a well-dressed green salad.
Serves 4 greedy or 6 normal people

TIPS: Unless meringues are beige on the outside and tacky on the inside, they're not!

LIKES: My wife's Spaghetti Carbonara. Bouillabaisse.

DISLIKES: Figs, camembert cheese.

CULINARY DISASTERS: My wife had one – she used, unknowingly, a pre-packed *sweet* pastry on a steak and kidney pie. Eight faces behaved very well on the first mouthful – by the second, laughter was continuous.

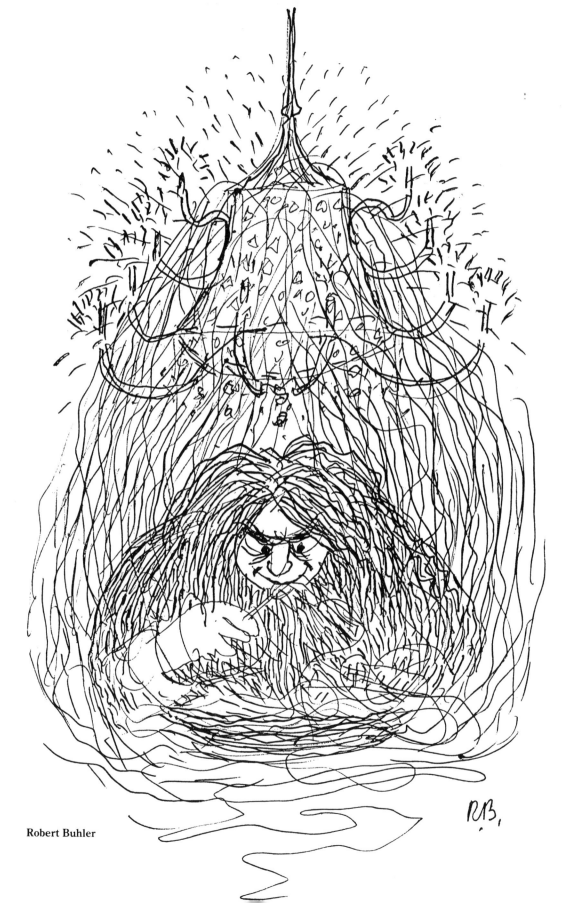

Robert Buhler

FILLET OF PORK HONGROISE

Molly Hardwick
Writer

Not difficult or time-consuming to prepare, and can be assembled the day before and pre-heated, with cream and mushrooms added just before serving.

2–3 pork fillets, about 1½–2lb (675–900g) (some butchers suggest pork leg)
1½oz (40g) butter
2 shallots or 1 small onion
1dssp paprika
1dssp flour
1tsp tomato purée
1 glass sherry
¼ pint (150ml) consommé, jellied
6oz (175g) button mushrooms
1 level dssp cornflour
1 small carton thick cream

Cut fillets into 2in (10cm) pieces, sauté briskly in very hot butter until just coloured. I use a heavy iron frying pan. Draw aside, remove pork to a warmed plate, add shallots/onion, very finely chopped, to the juices in the pan, with the paprika. Cook on low heat for 1–2 minutes. Stir in flour, tomato purée and add sherry and consommé. Stir till boiling, season, replace pork, cover pan and simmer gently for 30–40 minutes until tender. Five minutes before you judge the pork to be cooked through, draw aside pan, add mushrooms whole, and the cornflour mixed to a liquid with 2–3tbsp of cold water. Return to heat to complete cooking. Just before serving stir in the cream, mix well and serve very hot.

I use a hostess trolley, prepare the main dish early and add the cream absolutely at the last minute. This used to be an expensive dish, but somehow it doesn't seem so now. I can get the pork at Safeways easily enough. I do trim it myself to remove fat. It sounds elaborate, but it's enjoyable to prepare and it certainly works. Guests have asked for a spoon to finish the delicious gravy.
Serves 4

TIPS: Add the white of an egg when whipping cream; it makes it lighter and go further.

Salad & Vegetable Dishes

POMMES DE TERRE PAYSAN

Joan Collins
Actress

My favourite dish, otherwise known as Peasant Potatoes – though the average peasant can't afford it! It is simple to make, for the working girl who has got lots of money and not much time.

8 medium-sized potatoes
Butter
Beluga or any other caviar you can
    afford
Sour cream

Quickly scrub the potatoes (don't forget to put your rubber gloves on so you don't ruin your manicure). Put the potatoes in the microwave for approximately 9 minutes on High. Stick a fork in to see whether they are done. If you don't have a microwave, put in the oven at gas mark 6, 400°F (200°C) for 1 hour. Take out. Put out your most beautiful Wedgwood dishes; slit the potatoes in half and put a small pat of butter on each half, followed by a large tablespoon of caviar. As an alternative, you can throw a large tablespoon of sour cream on top of the caviar.

    Delish and bound to cause rave reviews!
Serves 8

Tony Husband

TIPS: Never put your hand on those new-fangled stoves. Just because it doesn't look red doesn't mean it can't burn you!

LIKES: Having somebody else do it for me.

DISLIKES: Cottage cheese, raw carrots, cooked tomatoes.

POMME DE TERRE CRYÈRE

Barry Cryer
Comedy writer

1 potato
Butter
Salt and pepper
Parsley, chopped
Onion, grated

Heat oven to gas mark 6, 400°F (200°C) or wrap the potato in three or four thicknesses of foil and put in the fire – *not the hottest part*. This is good for Bonfire Night or when Dad's burning VAT forms. Wash the skin. The potato's, not yours. Prick it with a fork and smear it with a little butter (a small goat) on a piece of paper. Put it on a rack in the centre of the oven. Test after 45 minutes (*Top of the Pops* and half of *Eastenders*; or if two small potatoes, just *Top of the Pops*). When your fork goes in easily, it's done.

Take it out of the oven . . . aaaaah! Use a cloth, silly. Cut the top off like a boiled egg. Scoop out the innards into a bowl. Add butter or margarine, a pinch of salt and a few shakes of pepper. Chopped parsley, grated onion or even chocolate mousse will add to the flavour. Mash it with a fork and taste. Spoon the mixture back into the skin and put the lid on. EAT!!!
Serves 1

POTATO GRIDDLE CAKES (Raggmunkar)

Dame Beryl Grey
Former Prima Ballerina

This is a Swedish recipe.

1 egg (optional)
2 cups milk
1¼ cups flour
1½lb (675g) potatoes
1tsp salt
Dash of white pepper
1tsp sugar
To fry: butter or lard

Beat egg and a little of the milk, then add flour and remaining milk alternately while beating. Allow to stand (2 hours if possible). Wash, peel and grate the potatoes, add to the batter and beat thoroughly. Season with salt and pepper and add sugar. Heat a griddle or frying pan, grease and cover with a thin layer of batter. When brown on both sides and crisp at the edges, place on a hot platter. Serve at once with either fried pork or lingonberries (cranberries – which we always eat with it).
Serves 4

TIPS: A pinch of bicarbonate when cooking rhubarb, apricots, blackberries etc, means you won't have to use as much sugar as usual.

POTATO LATKES

Claire Rayner
Writer and 'Agony Aunt'

Very fattening, very delicious and therefore not to be eaten too often!

About 2lb (1kg) potatoes, grated
1 large onion, grated
2 beaten eggs
Salt
Pepper
Flour

Use grated raw potato, and add grated raw onion. The potato must be left standing in a colander for about an hour, to let the excess liquid drain out. It will blacken a little, but that doesn't matter. Then press the rest of the liquid out and mix the onion and potato together, with beaten eggs, lots of salt and pepper and, if it's a bit sloppy, a little flour. In a heavy pan, heat oil till it smokes and drop in spoonfuls of the mixture. They'll fluff up, but also look ragged. Turn them and flatten them a little if necessary, and when they are golden brown, drain on kitchen paper and eat hot.

For a variation, the mixture can be piled into a buttered oven dish and baked in a hot oven gas mark 7, 425°F (220°C) for about 45 minutes, or till it's firm and golden brown. This way is rather heavier but just as delicious, and makes a change from roast potatoes with the Sunday joint.
Makes 12–18

TIPS: Only ever cook what you like eating; if you don't enjoy it then you won't be able to make it taste right, and then the people you're cooking for won't like it either.

DISLIKES: I hate cooking anything that has to be done in umpteen different stages. It gets very boring if you have to keep coming back to it hours later to turn it over in the marinade or twiddle with the dressing. I like to start, get on with it and eat it!

SPINACH PASTRY SNAKE

Anna Roden
Daughter of cookery writer
Claudia Roden

This is my favourite dish for parties, either as an hors d'oeuvre or as part of a buffet. It originates from the Ottoman Empire.

4lb (2kg) fresh spinach *or* **2lb (1kg) leaf spinach**
2tbsp oil
1lb (450g) cottage or curd cheese
10oz (275g) mature Cheddar cheese, grated
2 eggs, lightly beaten
1 bunch spring onions, chopped
¼tsp nutmeg
Salt and pepper
2oz (50g) butter
8oz (225g) filo or strudel pastry

Wash the spinach and remove the stems, then drain well and cook the leaves in their own juice by putting them on low heat in a large saucepan with the oil, stirring until they crumble into a soft mass. Alternative-ly, defrost the frozen spinach and squeeze out all the water. Drain well and put into a large bowl with the cottage or curd cheese, Cheddar cheese, eggs, spring onions, nut-meg, salt and pepper, and mix thoroughly.

Melt the butter and grease a tart or flan dish. Take the filo sheets out of their wrap when you are ready to use them, in a pile, so that they do not dry out. Brush each sheet with melted butter, put a row of the spinach filling an inch from the longer edge and roll up. Lift the rolls carefully on to the dish, crumpling them slightly, like an accordion. Fit them comfortably, without tearing, into a coiled snake shape so that they cover the base of the dish.

Brush the top with melted butter and bake in a pre-heated oven, gas mark 5, 375°F (190°C), for about 45 minutes, or until crisp and lightly browned. Serve hot.
Serves 8 as an hors d'oeuvre, but many more as part of a buffet.

Reg Smythe

73

SAVOURY CAULIFLOWER

Sylvia Syms
Actress

Large cauliflower
1 pint (600ml) milk
2oz (50g) butter or margarine
2oz (50g) flour
2 large onions, finely sliced
Oil and butter for frying
4oz (100g) grated cheese

Separate cauliflower into florets and cook lightly in boiling water, so that it's still crisp. Make a white sauce by whisking together the milk, butter or margarine and flour over a gentle heat until thickened. Fry the onions in oil and butter till transparent but not brown. Put the onions and sauce into a blender till thick and smooth. Place the cauliflower in a buttered oven dish, pour the white sauce over it and top with the grated cheese. Slowly brown under the grill till the cheese bubbles. Serve with a green peasant salad: lettuce or spinach leaves with lovage, chives and mint in a French dressing.

This dish can always be expanded by adding chopped ham (place it under the white sauce on top of the cauliflower), hard-boiled eggs (chopped) or any leftovers of savoury sausage, bacon etc.
Serves 2

COURGETTES WITH CREAM AND ROSEMARY

Lady Carrington
Wife of Lord Carrington, Secretary General of NATO

1½lb (675g) small courgettes
3oz (75g) butter
4oz (100g) double or whipping cream
4in (10cm) sprig of rosemary
Salt and pepper

Cut the unpeeled courgettes into thick diagonal slices. Blanch them in boiling salted water for about 5 minutes. Drain them well and put them back into the pan with the butter. Cover closely and leave them to finish cooking over a gentle heat. The courgettes must not brown or stick to the pan, so shake them from time to time. When they are tender, stir in the cream and rosemary and leave to simmer for another 5 minutes. Turn the courgettes fairly often, so that they are coated with the sauce and delicately flavoured with the rosemary. Fish out the sprig of rosemary before serving.

Other herbs can be substituted – parsley, chives, tarragon, fennel – but rosemary is best.
Serves 2

TIPS: Try chopped Chinese leaves instead of lettuce in salads and sandwiches. They have a much more interesting taste and don't curl up as fast.

MOROCCAN SALAD – TABOULI

Julie Christie
Actress

This is a very quick summer salad (when in season) which always impresses.

8oz (225g) cracked wheat (burghul)
1–2 cups fresh mint leaves
1–2 cups fresh parsley
2–3tbsp cold-pressed
   olive oil
2–3tbsp fresh lemon juice
} according to taste
Large handful almonds (they don't need to be peeled)
Large handful raisins
Plenty of ground black pepper
Salt to taste
Ground cumin
2–3 spring onions
¼ cucumber
2 tomatoes (optional)

About 1–1½ hours before preparing the salad, put grain in a bowl and cover with water. Leave it to absorb. If the water gets absorbed too quickly, add a little more. After about ½ hour it should be soft enough to eat.

To prepare salad: Chop mint leaves, parsley and add to grain, olive oil and lemon. Mix well. Boil a little water and throw in almonds for 3–4 minutes. Put raisins in a little water to soak. Cool almonds with cold water, chop in half, and add to grain. Generously sprinkle cumin over it. Add 2–3 chopped spring onions, and ¼ cucumber chopped into small cubes. Chopped tomatoes can also be added. Add soaked raisins, salt and pepper, mix well. Enjoy!
Serves 4

LIKES: Working around the restrictions of vegetables that are in season; using all that you can see in gardens and hedgerows as they appear gives me a feeling of being part of the seasonal rhythm of the year. Eating the food I've cooked – and other people's appreciation of food I've cooked. And trying to reconstruct delicious dishes I've tasted on my travels around the world.

DISLIKES: Processed foods (tins, packets etc). I feel I'm not eating real food, just lies constructed by chemical multi-nationals. Bad for the digestion.

GIRLS' SUMMER SALAD

Susan Hampshire
Actress

On a bed of lettuce or chicory:
1 banana, chopped
2 carrots, grated
2 tomatoes, sliced
Handful of raisins
Cottage cheese or mild goat's cheese
Pineapple or strawberries
6 almonds
Grated ginger root (optional)

Dressing:
Chopped chives and parsley
Walnut oil
1tsp lemon juice or cider vinegar
Onion salt to taste
Ground pepper

Arrange all the ingredients on the bed of lettuce or chicory. Grate the ginger root (if used) on to the cheese. Pour the dressing over.
Serves 2

CHAMP

Jeremy Irons
Actor

10 spring onions, or 2 leeks, cooked in ½ cup milk
1½lb (675g) freshly cooked mashed potatoes
Salt and pepper
4tbsp melted butter

Cook the chopped spring onions, green part as well as white, in the milk. Drain and keep the milk. Mash the potatoes, season to taste and add the spring onions. Beat well together and add enough hot milk to make the dish creamy and smooth. Place mixture in a deep, warmed dish, making a well in the centre and pour the hot, melted butter into the well. The dry potato should be dipped in the pool of butter when serving.

CHAMP can also be made with chopped parsley, chives, young nettle tops or young green peas. In the latter case, the peas are kept whole and added last. For a supper dish, scrambled eggs are often served in the centre; sprinkled with chopped parsley, it will kindle the coldest heart.
Serves 4

TIPS: Use walnut oil to dress salads; it's expensive but tastes superb.

ALMOND AND MUSHROOM BAKE

Anneka Rice
Broadcaster

6oz (175g) ground almonds
6oz (175g) wholemeal breadcrumbs
6oz (175g) button mushrooms
6oz (175g) carrots
1 onion
1 clove garlic
1tsp olive oil
2tbsp fresh chopped parsley
¾tsp dried thyme
Freshly ground black pepper
2 free-range eggs
2tbsp vegetable stock

Place the ground almonds in a large mixing bowl and stir in the breadcrumbs. Wipe the mushrooms and chop finely. Scrub the carrots and grate finely. Mix the mushrooms and carrots into the breadcrumb mixture. Finely chop the onion, garlic and celery and cook over a low heat in the oil for 3 minutes without browning. Add to the bowl with the parsley, thyme and pepper. Beat the eggs and pour on to the mixture with the stock. Mix in thoroughly to bind the mixture. Oil a 2lb (1kg) loaf tin and place the mixture inside, pressing down firmly. Cover with foil and put back in the centre of a pre-heated oven at gas mark 5, 375°F (190°C) for 25 minutes. Remove foil and cook for a further 10 minutes uncovered. Serve either hot or cold.
Serves 4

LIKES: The smells . . . particularly bread and cakes! Sometimes I put a drop of vanilla essence into a warm oven to make the kitchen smell like I'm a real expert.

DISLIKES: Peeling vegetables and washing up.

CULINARY DISASTERS: The first Chicken Kiev I ever made was a disaster. The recipe told me to use a clove of garlic – and I thought this meant the whole bulb! The smell nearly knocked everyone out!

77

VEGETABLE LASAGNE

Clare Francis
Writer and round-the-world
yachtswoman

2tbsp oil
1 large onion, sliced
1½ green peppers, sliced
8oz (225g) mushrooms, sliced
Grated carrots (optional)
1lb (450g) aubergines, sliced
8oz (225g) courgettes, sliced
Tomato purée
1 tin kidney beans
1 medium tin tomatoes
Salt and pepper
Herbs
Fresh basil if available
½ pint (300ml) stock
8oz (225g) pasta
Béchamel sauce
Grated cheese – Cheddar or Mozarella

Heat 2tbsp oil in a frying pan, and gently cook onions, peppers and mushrooms for about 10 minutes, plus carrots if you wish. Meanwhile, steam aubergines and courgettes for about 10 minutes. Add tomato purée to fried vegetables and mix well. Add tinned kidney beans, tomatoes, freshly steamed vegetables, seasoning, herbs and stock. Stir gently and simmer for 5–10 minutes. Take freshly cooked pasta (or pre-cooked variety) and starting with the tomato sauce, alternate with layers of pasta, finishing with a layer of sauce.

Top the dish with Béchamel sauce and grated Cheddar cheese or Mozarella. Cook in oven for 20–25 minutes at gas mark 6, 400°F (200°C).
Serves 4–6

DISLIKES: I must be the only person in the world who does not like French cooking. I hate their lack of vegetables and very over-rich sauces. It is Italian cooking for me every time.

CULINARY DISASTERS: My culinary disasters are numerous – one was actually nailed up over my kitchen door for many years.

CARROTT CURRY

Jasper Carrott
Comedian

4tbsp peanut oil or melted butter
1½tsp salt
1½tsp turmeric
1tbsp cumin seeds
½tsp cinnamon
1tsp coriander, ground
4 carrots, sliced
3 large potatoes, diced
2 medium-sized onions, sliced
1 small swede, diced
¾ pint (425ml) water
¼ pint (150ml) plain yogurt
5oz (150g) frozen peas, defrosted

Heat the oil or butter in a large saucepan; when it is warm add all the spices. Simmer for about 3 minutes, then add all the vegetables, stirring immediately to coat them with the spices. Keep stirring for about 5 minutes on a low heat. Put the water in, and simmer all the ingredients for about ½ hour, stirring occasionally. If the vegetables are tender, stir in the yogurt and the peas. Cook for about another 10 minutes on a lowish heat. Serve with saffron rice.
Serves 4

JAPANESE VEGETABLES

Bruce Forsyth
All-round entertainer

I am very fond of Japanese food, particularly for the way in which vegetables are not overcooked. The following recipe is incredibly simple but nonetheless delicious.

In a wok, melt a little butter and add a crushed clove of garlic; then stir-fry an equal amount of bean sprouts and mange-tout peas for just a couple of minutes. Season to taste with either salt and pepper or a dash of soy sauce.

CHEESE AND SWEET CORN SOUFFLÉ

Geoffrey Smith
Gardening writer and broadcaster

This makes a delicious, light meal served with roast potatoes and green peas or other vegetables.

2oz (50g) butter
2oz (50g) plain flour
½tsp salt
¾ pint (450ml) milk
4oz (100g) grated Cheddar cheese
3 eggs
12oz (350g) tin sweetcorn

Make a sauce by melting butter in saucepan and stirring in the flour – cook for 1 minute. Add salt and milk and cook until thick. Allow to cool a little, then add grated cheese. Separate the egg yolks from the whites and add the yolks to the mixture, together with the drained sweetcorn. Lastly, stir in the stiffly beaten whites of egg. Pour into four lightly greased individual soufflé dishes. Place in a tray with water, in the bottom of oven at gas mark 4, 350°F (180°C), for approximately 50 minutes.
Serves 4

TIPS: Do not overcook vegetables, which should be freshly gathered.

DISLIKES: Mincemeat and treacle pudding. A relic of boarding-school days.

CULINARY DISASTERS: An attempt at making light individual sponge cakes which came out as biscuits. My wife gave birth the day after witnessing this culinary feat.

MYSTERY POTATO

Eamonn Andrews
Broadcaster

First of all, get nice, large, old potatoes – it won't work with new ones – and scrub them as clean as a whistle; but don't take off the skins. Heat up your oven, say to about gas mark 6, 400°F (200°C). Dry the potatoes and stab them well with a fork. Whatever you do, don't forget the stabbing, because if you don't prick those potatoes, you'll have a mighty explosion and you'll not be the most popular person in the house by the time somebody has scraped off potato fragments from all round the oven.

Now you've plenty of time to think of your mystery filling. Leave the potatoes in there for an hour or so till the skin is crackling and crispy. When they're done, you'll need a cloth or oven gloves to handle them. Try and split each one down the middle. Mash in a tiny blob of butter, if you're not dieting, or a drop of milk if you are, and then almost anything you like. Try a spoonful or so of chopped onion or grated cheese. You can even have scrambled egg or some tinned salmon – which isn't at all bad. And don't forget to eat the skins afterwards.

If you get very ambitious, you can always split the baked potato right down the middle, scoop out the inside and mix with your favourite filling. Then refill each half, perhaps popping it under the grill for a final heat.

One potato per person, two for a big appetite.

Glen Baxter

IT WAS THE FOURTH TIME THAT DADDY HAD
FALLEN FOR THE EXPLODING FORK ROUTINE...

Desserts

BAKED BANANAS

Glenda Jackson
Actress

6 bananas
½ cup fresh orange juice
2tbsp rum or brandy
2–3tbsp brown sugar
½tsp nutmeg
½tsp cinnamon
½oz (15g) butter
Cream for serving

Split bananas in half and place in buttered baking dish. Mix orange juice and rum with sugar and spices and pour over the bananas. Dot with butter and bake at gas mark 4, 350°F (180°C) for 20 minutes. Serve hot with cream.
Serves 6

JAM PANCAKES

Lord Jakobovits
Chief Rabbi

2 eggs
¼ glass milk
2tbsp flour
1 pinch of salt
Strawberry jam (or any jam that you choose)
Oil

Heat oil in flat frying pan. Beat eggs, milk, flour and salt to a very light mixture. Spread thinly on hot, oily pan. Watch carefully. Turn upside down. When fried on both sides, turn on to large plate and spread with jam. Roll into an appetising pancake. Enjoy!
Serves 2–4

TIPS: Fresh bread dipped into red wine is delicious.

DISLIKES: Beetroot.

CULINARY DISASTERS: Cooking rice without water!

BURNT CREAMS WITH GINGER AND RASPBERRIES

Derek Nimmo
Actor

2 whole eggs
2 egg yolks
½ pint (300ml) single cream
1oz (25g) caster sugar
1 large piece stem ginger, finely
   chopped
1 level tsp gelatine crystals dissolved
   in 1tbsp boiling water
4oz (100g) fresh or defrosted frozen
   raspberries
Icing sugar for glazed topping
1 extra piece stem ginger, sliced into 6
   to garnish
Whipped cream (optional)

Beat the whole eggs and egg yolks. Bring the cream, sugar and chopped ginger to the boil, pour over the eggs, whisking all the time. Mix in the small amount of melted gelatine. Divide the raspberries evenly between 6 ramekins. Pour over the cream mixture and leave to cool and set.

Pre-heat the grill to spanking hot. Dredge the top of the creams with a good ⅛in (0.25cm) cushion of icing sugar. Wipe the edges clean. Stand the ramekins in a tin of ice-cold water, slide this under the grill and let the sugar melt to a good, dark caramel colour. Cool, but do not refrigerate again as this will soften the crisp layer of caramel. Decorate with a slice of stem ginger and/or a blob of whipped cream.
Serves 6

TIPS: Eat radishes the French way – with a little butter spread on them.

Glen Baxter

OUR HEARTS SANK AS THE CHILLING
HIGHLIGHT OF THE FESTIVE ORDEAL
LUMBERED INTO VIEW...

BANANAS FOSTER

Shaw Taylor
Television presenter

A rich, tasty dessert that is not too filling.

2oz (50g) butter
3oz (75g) dark brown sugar
½tsp cinnamon
4fl oz (100ml) rum
4 bananas cut into blocks
4 portions of ice cream

Melt butter, add sugar and cinnamon and half the rum. Stir until melted. Add bananas and cook for one minute. Add rest of rum, and flambé. Spoon on to dish of ice cream.
Serves 4

CHOCOLATE POTS

Lady Forte
Wife of Lord Forte,
Chairman of
Trusthouse Forte

6oz (175g) Meunier chocolate
½ pint (300ml) single cream
1 egg
½tsp vanilla essence
Extra grated chocolate for decoration

Break chocolate into pieces and put into container of an electric blender. Heat cream in a saucepan until boiling point and pour it on to the chocolate. Cover with blender lid, switch on and blend until smooth. Add egg and vanilla essence and blend again for a few moments. Pour into 6 individual pots. Chill overnight. Sprinkle grated chocolate and serve with a little cream.
Serves 6

TIPS: The puréed flesh of a ripe mango, mixed with water, crushed ice and a little sugar to taste, makes an unusual and refreshing summer drink.

RHUBARB AND GINGER CRUMBLE

Mary Peters
Former athlete

2lb (1kg) rhubarb, cut into pieces
1 cooking apple, peeled, cored and
   chopped
2tsp ground ginger
2oz (50g) brown sugar
1oz (25g) crystallised ginger, chopped

Topping:
4oz (100g) wholewheat flour
2oz (50g) brown sugar
3oz (75g) butter
1tbsp clear honey

Pre-heat oven to gas mark 4, 350°F (180°C). Arrange the rhubarb and apple in a well-greased, oven-proof dish, sprinkle over the ginger, sugar and crystallised ginger.

To make the topping, mix the flour and sugar together. Rub in the butter until the mixture resembles fine breadcrumbs. Stir in the honey. Bake in pre-heated oven for 45 minutes, or until the top is golden and crisp.

Serves 4

Reg Smythe

TIPS: When boiling vegetables, put a knob of butter in the water to prevent them boiling over.

CULINARY DISASTERS: Adding coffee essence instead of gravy browning to the meat stock – what a lovely Sunday lunch!

BANANA MERINGUE

Barry Took
Writer and broadcaster

6 bananas
2oz (50g) butter or Flora
1tsp ground cinnamon
3 eggs, separated
2oz (50g) soft brown sugar
1tbsp rum
3oz (75g) caster sugar

Cut the bananas into half and then split each half lengthways. Fry in butter or Flora until golden brown, then place in a lightly buttered oven-proof dish and sprinkle with cinnamon.

Separate the eggs and put yolks into a bowl over a saucepan of hot water. Add the brown sugar and heat gently, stirring until the mixture thickens. Do not allow to boil. Stir in rum and pour mixture over bananas.

Whisk the egg whites until stiff and fold in the caster sugar. Pile on top of ingredients in dish and bake in oven gas mark 2, 300°F (150°C) for 35 minutes until the meringue is browned.
Serves 6

PORTUGUESE BREAD MOUNTAIN

Leslie Crowther
Comedian and game show host

8oz (225g) white bread (without crusts)
½ pint (300ml) red wine
8oz (225g) sugar
Thinly peeled rind of ½ a lemon
½tsp cinnamon
3 eggs, separated
Fat for frying
Apricot jam
6oz (175g) caster sugar

Cut the bread into fingers and put into a bowl. Put the wine, sugar, lemon peel and cinnamon into a small pan and bring to the boil. Beat the egg yolks over a low heat until thick, then add the wine, stirring all the time. Strain over the bread and leave for about 15 minutes. With great care, brown the fingers in hot fat. When cold, spread with jam. Pile into a heap on a dish. Whisk egg whites and most of the caster sugar, reserving some to sprinkle over the top. Cover bread with whisked eggs and sugar. Bake in a slow oven gas mark 2, 300°F (150°C) until the meringue is a light golden brown.
Serves 4–6

TIPS: Don't use freshly laid eggs when making meringues – the whites won't fluff up.

PORT AND CLARET JELLY

Ian Carmichael
Actor

¾ pint (450ml) water
8oz (225g) sugar
Juice and rind of 2 lemons
Stick of cinnamon
6 cloves
¾ pint (450ml) claret
½ pint (300ml) port
Drop of brandy
1½oz (40g) gelatine (let down with a
    little claret)
Clotted cream

In a saucepan, dissolve sugar in water with juice and rind of lemons, cloves and cinnamon. Add dissolved gelatine, and allow to simmer for several minutes. *Don't allow to boil*. Pour through sieve into port and claret, add brandy, and stir well. Leave to set in individual dishes or wine glasses. Serve with a whirl of clotted cream on top.
Serves 4–6

BROWN BREAD ICE CREAM

Nanette Newman
Actress and author

3oz (75g) brown breadcrumbs
2oz (50g) demerara sugar
4 eggs, separated
½ pint (300ml) double cream
2oz (50g) caster sugar

Mix the breadcrumbs and demerara sugar together and then grill them on the lowest setting until brown and crunchy (make sure they don't burn). Leave to cool.
    Lightly beat the egg yolks. Whisk the double cream until thick. Finally, whisk the egg whites to soft peaks and gradually whisk in the caster sugar until glossy. Fold all the ingredients together and freeze in a suitable container or an ice-cream mould.
Serves 6

Quentin Blake

BANANA AND DATE LAYER PUDDING

Libby Purves
Broadcaster and journalist

Sir Hugh Casson

This is a very, very, very easy pudding to make, also very fattening, but everyone eats it with relish and thinks it took you trouble to make.

Bananas
Dates
Double cream
Brown sugar (optional)

Take some bananas, slice them up. Take some dates (fresh or boxed) and stone them. Pile alternate layers of bananas and dates in a very pretty cut-glass trifle dish, until it is full. Pour double cream over the lot until it is just covered. Shove it in the fridge, covered, for several hours. If you want to show off, just before serving you can sprinkle it with brown sugar and flash it under a very hot grill. Just don't blame me if the glass bowl cracks: some do, some don't . . .

TIPS: Always put the lid on before you heat up popcorn, or it will stick to the light-fittings.

LIKES: The smell of cooking. That's *all* I like about it.

DISLIKES: The curdling of all my sauces, always.

CULINARY DISASTERS: Using a left-over half-bottle of white wine in a chicken casserole. Not only was it sweet as candy floss, it was fizzy, too. Stew too nasty to eat so we froze it for six months. It was still nasty so I put curry powder in, and it was EVEN WORSE.

MOTHER OF ALI (Om Ali)

Claudia Roden
Cookery writer

This creamy Egyptian dessert is a kind of bread pudding. In the villages it is made with a flat, pitta-type bread, and in the cities with pastry such as filo.

5 sheets of filo weighing about 3¾oz (100g)
1tbsp butter, melted
5oz (150g) mixed nuts such as pistachios, almonds, hazelnuts and walnuts, coarsely chopped
2oz (50g) raisins
1 pint (1 litre) milk
4tbsp sugar or to taste
½ pint (300ml) double cream

Brush the sheets of filo with butter and put them in a very high gas mark 9, 475°F (240°C) oven on separate shelves, or loosely one on top of the other for 3 or 4 minutes or until they are crisp and very slightly golden.

When they are cool enough, break them with your hands into a baking dish or into small individual bowls, sprinkle with nuts and raisins and mix well. Heat the milk with the sugar and add the cream, then pour over the filo and nut mixture. Bake in a gas mark 4, 350°F (180°C) oven for 20–30 minutes until browned. Serve hot.

Serves 6

MELON SURPRISE

David Bedford
Former athlete

1 melon – any kind except water melon
1 grapefruit
1 orange or 2 tangerines
1 apple
4oz (100g) green or black grapes, stoned
4oz (100g) red cherries, stoned
Cointreau or Martini

Cut top off melon. Cut base so that it can stand in fridge. Scoop out inside. Clean and prepare fruit – chop into small pieces. Mix fruit with melon and pack into melon skin. Add Cointreau or Martini to taste. Put lid back on and decorate according to occasion – eg holly sprigs for Christmas, cocktail accessories or even sparklers.

As a variation, put whipped cream on top of melon. Add hats or funny faces for children or even adults' parties.

Note: Be conservative with alcohol for children's parties!!!

Serves 4–6

TIPS: When chopping mint for mint sauce, sprinkle it with sugar and salt to make the task easier and quicker.

MOCHA MOUSSE

Rt Hon Nigel Lawson, MP
Chancellor of the Exchequer

5oz (150g) dark chocolate
1tbsp instant coffee granules
2tbsp water
4 eggs, separated
Single cream to serve

Keeping back one square of chocolate, melt the rest in a bowl standing in a pan of nearly boiling water. Dissolve the coffee granules in 2tbsp of boiling water (or, for a richer flavour, use rum) and mix into the melted chocolate. Separate the eggs and add the yolks to the mixture, one by one, beating well in between. Whip the egg whites in a bowl until stiff, but not dry, and gradually fold into the chocolate mixture, taking care to keep the mixture light and fluffy. Turn this out into a serving dish or into individual dishes, and refrigerate for at least 2 hours before serving. Serve with single cream and decorate with grated chocolate.
Serves 4

QUICK SPLIT

Jeff Wayne
Composer and record producer

This dish was created by my three children, Anna-Marie (9), Jemma (7) and Zebidiah (2). It is a tried and tested winner. I know because I had to clean up afterwards!

2 bananas
Whipping cream
1 chocolate flake
Hundreds and thousands
Ice cream

Cut the bananas in half, lengthways.
   Squeeze the whipped cream over the bananas.
   Stick the flake in the bananas.
   Sprinkle the hundreds and thousands over it.
   Scoop the ice cream out onto the Quick Split.
Serves 2

TIPS: Cheat! Buy homemade cakes from local farmshops or church bazaars and say you baked them yourself!

FRUIT CLAFOUTIS

Jane Asher
Actress and author

You can make this as sophisticated or as simple as you choose, depending on the fruit you put into it. It would be excellent with fresh peaches, mangoes or grapes, or as a plainer but equally good family dish with apples or pears.

14oz (400g) tin pitted black cherries
8oz (225g) tin apricots
3 eggs
4oz (100g) caster sugar
2oz (50g) flour
½ pint (300ml) milk
¼ pint (150ml) double cream
Icing sugar to serve

Heat the oven to gas mark 5, 375°F (190°C). Drain the cherries and apricots and place them in an oven-proof dish. Whisk the eggs and caster sugar in a bowl until light and fluffy, then sift in the flour and whisk again until the mixture is smooth.

Gradually whisk in the milk and cream. Pour this batter over the fruit and cook in the pre-heated oven for 45 minutes, or until it is just set and the top is golden brown. You can serve immediately, or keep it warm in a low oven until ready to serve. Immediately before serving, sprinkle the top with sieved icing sugar. It is also delicious cold.
Serves 6

TIPS: Don't feel guilty – cut corners whenever you can if you're busy (use good 'mixes', frozen pastry etc).

LIKES: The satisfaction of putting something attractive and delicious and hopefully reasonably healthy on the table and seeing it enjoyed.

DISLIKES: The clearing-up; peeling potatoes; peeling garlic; having to cook for the daily family meals if I'm not in the mood!

BREAD AND BUTTER PUDDING (1)

Melvyn Bragg
Writer and TV arts presenter

6 slices white bread
1¼oz (30g) butter
2oz (50g) sultanas
1¼ pints (750ml) milk
3 medium eggs (beaten)
2oz (50g) caster sugar

Sandwich bread with butter. Cut into 2in (5cm) pieces. Butter a serving dish. Layer bread with sultanas in dish. Warm milk and mix with beaten eggs and sugar. Pour over bread and leave to soak for 10 minutes. Bake for 40 minutes at gas mark 3, 325°F (160°C) until soft and golden.
Serves 4

BREAD AND BUTTER PUDDING (2)

Lord Brabourne
Film producer

10 slices stale white bread
6oz (175g) mixed dried fruit
1oz (25g) mixed peel
3oz (75g) soft brown sugar
4tsp mixed spice
2oz (50g) soft butter
Caster sugar

Soak the bread in cold water. Squeeze dry with your hands to expel as much water as possible, then beat with a fork to remove any lumps. Add the remaining ingredients and mix thoroughly. Put the mixture into a well-greased cake tin and bake at gas mark 5, 375°F (190°C) for 1½–2 hours. Turn out, sprinkle liberally with caster sugar and serve hot with custard or cold with cream.
Serves 6

TIPS: To remove hairs from strawberries, rinse in cold water using a pinch of salt.

PEARS IN RED WINE

Rt Hon
Margaret Thatcher, MP
The Prime Minister

5oz (150g) lump sugar
¼ pint (150ml) water
¼ pint (150ml) red wine
  (claret/burgundy)
Strip of lemon rind
Small piece of stick cinnamon
5–6 ripe dessert pears
1tsp arrowroot

To make syrup: dissolve sugar, water, wine and flavourings slowly in a pan. Bring to boil for 1 minute.

Keeping stalks on pears, remove peel and the eye from each base and carefully take out the core, using an apple corer. Keeping the pears covered, poach gently in the syrup, until tender. Even if the pears are ripe, you must allow at least 20–30 minutes to prevent discoloration. Remove pears and strain syrup, which should be reduced to ½ pint (300ml) in the cooking. Mix the arrowroot with a little water and thicken the syrup. Arrange pears in a serving dish and spoon over the sauce. Serve cold with whipped cream.
Serves 5–6

TIPS: 'Mrs Thatcher prefers to use a copper mixing bowl. Although cooks have used them over the centuries, today science can provide reasons which underline that preference. Because of their molecular structure you will find, for example, that egg whites "peak" more readily to produce excellent meringues.'
                    (Press Office, 10 Downing Street)

STRAWBERRIES À LA WENDY

Lulu
Singer and actress

6–8 sugar cubes
1 large orange
1 small glass of brandy
1lb (450g) of strawberries, sliced
Single cream for serving

Rub the sugar cubes over the orange rind until the oil from the rind has soaked into the cubes. Crush the cubes (with a pestle and mortar if available). Squeeze the orange and add the juice to the brandy and crushed sugar cubes. Pour the mixture over the sliced strawberries. Cover and chill for 3 to 4 hours and serve with the cream.
Serves 4

John Anscomb   "Don't forget the fresh strawberries".

ZABAGLIONE

Alfred Marks
Actor and comedian

As a rule allow 1 egg yolk, 1 tablespoon of sugar, and 1–2 tablespoons of wine per person.

4 egg yolks
2oz (50g) caster sugar
4–6tbsp Marsala wine or sweet sherry
Sponge fingers

Put the egg yolks in a medium-sized mixing basin. Add the sugar and Marsala wine or sweet sherry to the egg yolks. Place the bowl over a saucepan half filled with simmering water, and whisk continuously over the heat until the mixture is thick and light. This takes about 5 minutes.

Remove from the heat and pour into four individual goblets. Serve with sponge fingers.
Serves 4

GLAZED FRUIT SPONGE FLAN

Rt Hon Kenneth Baker, MP
Secretary of State for Education

2 egg yolks
2oz (50g) sugar
1 egg white
1oz (25g) plain flour
½–¾ pint (300–450ml) milk
¼tsp vanilla essence
1 large bought sponge flan
1tsp lemon juice
1 banana
1 apple or some raspberries or grapes
1 kiwi fruit, if available
½ cup apricot jam or redcurrant jelly

In a pan whisk yolks and sugar, then add egg white until thick and pale. Gradually stir in the flour and then the milk, till smooth. Place pan in a larger pan of simmering water. Stir continually till it thickens. Simmer gently for 3 minutes, add vanilla. Cool a little and pour gently on to the flan. Prepare fruit – leave skin on apple. Squeeze lemon juice over apple and banana. Arrange in circle on the crème. Melt jam or jelly over gentle heat – sieve if necessary – and trickle over fruit to glaze.

Serve cold with cream.
Serves 10

TIPS: Wear goggles or large specs when pickling onions, to prevent your eyes watering.

MOCHA FUDGE PROFITEROLES
Fenton Bresler
Barrister and writer

¼ pint (150ml) milk and water in equal
   quantities
2oz (50g) butter
2oz (50g) plain flour
Pinch of salt
2 medium-sized eggs

Filling:
Small carton double cream
Brandy

Mocha fudge icing:
1½oz (40g) margarine
2oz (50g) carob buttons
4tsp instant coffee (diluted in 1tbsp of
   hot water)
4oz (100g) sieved icing sugar
2tbsp evaporated milk
½tsp vanilla essence

Put butter and liquid in a saucepan and bring slowly to the boil. Beat in the flour and salt until it forms a soft ball that doesn't stick to the saucepan. Once the mixture has cooled down a little, beat in the eggs – one at a time. Drop small teaspoons of the mixture onto a greased baking sheet. Bake at gas mark 6, 400°F (200°C) for about 20 minutes or until the profiteroles are golden brown and firm to the touch. Allow them to cool on a wire rack before cutting in half, filling with whipped cream and icing with mocha fudge. You can serve them as a dessert or for afternoon tea.
Cream filling:
Whip double cream until thick and flavour with a little brandy.
Mocha fudge icing:
Melt margarine, carob and coffee in a saucepan over a low heat. Then stir in icing sugar, evaporated milk and vanilla. Beat until smooth and glossy and then carefully coat each profiterole with a generous dollop. A bit messy but delicious!
Makes about 20

TIPS: You can try using carob as a substitute for chocolate in all sorts of cakes and puddings. It gives a delicious and slightly unusual flavour, and I kid myself that it makes calorie-laden recipes just a little healthier to eat!

RASPBERRY RICE CREAM

Janet Laurence
Cookery writer

A pudding for those who still love nursery food that will also please those whose tastes are rather more sophisticated. If you prefer, the cream can be omitted and skimmed rather than full cream milk used to cook the rice.

3oz (75g) short-grain or pudding rice, well washed
1 pint (600ml) milk, full cream is nicest
4oz (100g) vanilla sugar or caster sugar, and few drops vanilla essence
2 size-2 eggs, yolks separated from whites
2½fl oz (75ml) double cream
8oz (225g) raspberries, fresh or defrosted

Bring rice, milk and 2oz (50g) of the sugar to the boil, lower heat, cover and simmer very gently until rice is cooked. If milk is not completely absorbed, remove lid and cook a little longer. Beat the egg yolks until they increase in volume and pale slightly. Remove rice from heat, stir in yolks, then return to a very low heat and cook gently until mixture is slightly thickened. Cover with cling film and cool, or stir to prevent a skin forming. Whip cream until it will just hold its shape and fold into rice. Whip egg whites to stiff peak; whip in remaining sugar. Fold meringue mixture into rice. Finally, reserve a few nice raspberries for decoration, then carefully fold rest into rice. Place into four small dishes and garnish with reserved fruit.
Serves 4

Cakes & Biscuits

FRANKLIN

SPICY BUTTERMILK COFFEE CAKE

Steve Ovett
Athlete

2¼ cups plain flour
½tsp salt
2tsp cinnamon
4tsp ginger
1 cup brown sugar
¾ cup white sugar
¾ cup corn oil
1 cup chopped nuts
1tsp soda
1tsp baking powder
1 egg (beaten)
1 cup buttermilk

Mix together in a large bowl the flour, salt, 1tsp of cinnamon, ginger, both sugars, and corn oil. Remove ¾ cup of this mixture and to it add nuts and 1tsp cinnamon. Mix well and set this aside for the topping. To the remaining batter, add baking soda, baking powder, egg and buttermilk. Mix just to combine ingredients, no more. (Small lumps in batter are okay.) Pour batter into large, well-greased cake tin. Sprinkle the topping mixture over evenly. Bake at gas mark 4, 350°F (180°C) for 40–45 minutes.

Happy eating.

FLAPJACKS

Geoff Capes
Shot-putter

8oz (225g) wholemeal flour
4oz (100g) margarine
4oz (100g) brown sugar
4oz (100g) oats
3tbsp syrup
3oz (75g) raisins

Sieve the flour. Add the margarine to the flour and sieve through your fingers, to make a breadcrumb consistency. Add the sugar, oats and raisins. Mix in the syrup. Knead the mixture into a dough and roll out with a rolling pin. Place onto a greased baking tray and prick all over with a fork. Place in top half of the oven, gas mark 5, 375°F (190°C) for 20–25 minutes until a light brown. Leave to cool slightly and then cut into rectangles and serve.
Makes about 20

TIPS: Microwave sausages before frying them. This way the insides are done first and they are then finished off to a crispy skin in the frying-pan.

DISLIKES: Russian Beetroot Soup with raw egg in it!

CHOCOLATE RUM TORTE

Dulcie Gray
Actress and author

3 eggs
3oz (75g) caster sugar
1oz (25g) cocoa
2oz (50g) self-raising flour
2tbsp corn oil
¼ pint (150ml) double cream
3tbsp rum
3tbsp evaporated milk
4oz (100g) plain chocolate
Chocolate curls

Pre-heat oven to gas mark 4, 350°F (180°C). Line and grease a 7in (18cm) cake tin. Whisk the eggs and sugar together until you have a pale, thick mixture. Sift the cocoa and flour together, and fold it into the egg mixture with the corn oil. Turn it into the tin and bake for 40 minutes. Remove it and leave it to cool. Cut it in half across the middle. Whip the cream until it is soft. Fold in 2tbsp of the rum, and use to sandwich the cake together.

Heat the remaining rum (1tbsp) with the evaporated milk. Break the chocolate into pieces. Remove the rum and milk mixture from the heat. Stir in the chocolate until it has dissolved. Cool it until it is just warm, and is of good coating consistency – thinning it with more evaporated milk if necessary. Pour the icing over the cake, and decorate with chocolate curls.

With fresh cream, eat the cake soon, otherwise use rum-flavoured butter icing.

Maurice Dodd

TEISEN LAP

Sir Harry Secombe
Comedian and singer

Teisen means cake, and Lap means plate, so this is a Plate Cake. They are traditionally made all over Wales.

½ cup butter
1 heaped tbsp lard
2 cups flour
1 heaped tsp baking powder
½tsp nutmeg
½ cup sugar
1 cup mixed currants and seedless raisins or sultanas
2 eggs, well beaten
¼ pint (approx) cream, milk or buttermilk

Rub the fat into the flour and add the dry ingredients. Mix in the beaten eggs, and gradually add enough cream or milk to make a fairly soft mixture. Beat well, and either grease a shallow tin or plate and put the mixture in, or roll out to 1in (3.5cm) thickness on a floured table; cut into rounds and cook on a moderate bakestone or hotplate for about 15 minutes each side. If cooking in the shallow tin or plate, cook in a moderate oven gas mark 4, 350°F (180°C) for 20 minutes, then lower the heat to gas mark 1, 275°F (140°C) for about 40 minutes. Test with a skewer before removing from the oven, and turn out to cool on a wire rack.

BANANA, DATE AND HONEY CAKE

Mike Yarwood
Impressionist

4oz (100g) margarine
4oz (100g) soft brown sugar
1 egg
5oz (150g) ripe mashed banana (no skins)
2tbsp runny honey
6oz (175g) chopped dates
5oz (150g) wholemeal flour
5oz (150g) white self-raising flour
1tsp baking powder
Pinch of salt

Cream margarine and sugar together. Beat in egg. Add banana and honey and beat well. Stir in the dates. Mix flour, baking powder and salt together, and stir into creamed mixture. When well mixed, turn into a greased oblong tin 9in×5in×3in (22cm×12cm×7.5cm). Bake in the centre of oven, gas mark 3, 325°F (160°C) for about 1½ hours, or until centre of cake feels firm.
Delicious on its own or buttered.

TIPS: Any left-over hard-boiled egg yolks can be sieved into French dressing to make it extra creamy.

DARKEST PERUVIAN BISCUITS

Michael Bond
Creator of Paddington Bear

This is not really my favourite recipe, but Paddington is very fond of these biscuits. In fact he was keen for me to send you a recipe for marmalade sandwiches . . .

8oz (225g) butter
8oz (225g) dark soft brown sugar
4oz (100g) flour
1 egg

Cream butter and sugar together, mix in flour and add the egg, beating it in. Chill in refrigerator until the mixture can be cut cleanly with a knife. Drop little lumps of this paste onto buttered greaseproof paper on a baking sheet, allowing space between each drop for spreading. Bake for 15 minutes in the oven, pre-heated to gas mark 3, 325°F (160°C). Cool on a wire rack before removing from paper.
Makes about 24 biscuits

TIPS: To skin tomatoes, plunge them into boiling water and leave for about 20 seconds. Remove and plunge them straight into iced water. The skins will come away easily.

CULINARY DISASTERS: I once made some tea using water from an electric kettle which, unbeknown to me, had been previously used to boil a cabbage. It was during the war and I was working for the BBC. Tea was rationed, so I wasn't very popular. Moral: always fill the kettle with fresh water.

No. 56: Little Ones' Lunch

This week, *busy* mature student & mother-of-six, *Wendy Weber*, guides you through the favourite eating experience of her Under Sevens.....

Fizzy Drink:
Ingredients: ½ can per child carbonated drink

2. Pour contents into mug....

3. Place mouth over rim of mug to catch bubbles....

4. Take swig of contents. Hold in mouth until bubbles disappear...

5. Spit back into mug.

6. Repeat until reprimanded.

STOPPIT Benji!

Jelly 'n' ice cream:

2. Take mouthful of jelly....

3. Sloosh jelly between teeth until liquid....

4. Spit jelly juice back in bowl!.....

5. Repeat until all jelly reduced to liquid state....

6. Fold ice cream into jelly juice.

HOW REVOLTING!

That's ENOUGH!

© Posy Simmonds 1985

Cakes & Biscuits

Menu

Fizzy Drink

Noodles with Sauce

Stew, Mash, Peas

Jelly 'n' ice cream

Chocolate Digestive Biscuit

Wendy and husband, George, believe in feeding the younger members of their lively brood, SIMPLE, balanced meals.....

SIMPLE!? Haaa! That's a laugh!

Manda doesn't eat meat... He only eats peas and jelly...

Noodles with Sauce:

 2. Place noodle in mouth...

 Exhale, as if sounding the Last Trump....

 4. Repeat until reprimanded

For Godsake Manda! Stoppit!

Stew, Mash, Peas:

 2. Create gravy lake in Mash mountain

 3. Float peas in gravy lake...

 4. **Agitate** peas, mash, gravy into right old pigs' breakfast....

Disgusting MESS!! Will you just EAT up!

 5. Insert pea up nostril...

Chocolate Digestive Biscuits:

 2. Take a biscuit.....

 3. Lick off all the chocolate....

 4. Crumble the remains behind the radiator...

...! D'you understand, Tamsin? ...very naughty! ...had ENOUGH! ...silly! ...waste!...

Look, it's all better, Benji! It's out!

I've told you before...just DON'T put peas up there!

105

TORRONE MOLLE

Elizabeth David
Cookery writer

This excellent chocolate sweet needs barely a couple of minutes actual cooking and the rest of the preparation is of the utmost simplicity. The word *torrone* is Italian for all kinds of nougat, and *molle* means soft. In this recipe, which came well over thirty years ago from a Tuscan cook called Lina, the soft nougat is moulded in a tin and turned out when well-chilled.

6oz (175g) each of unsweetened cocoa, butter, sugar, ground almonds, plain *petit beurre* biscuits
1 whole egg and 1 yolk
A little sweet almond oil for the tin

Work the butter and cocoa together until you have a soft paste. Stir in the ground almonds. In a thick saucepan melt the sugar, moistened with a little water over a gentle heat. Add to the cocoa mixture. Beat in the whole egg and the egg yolk. Now break the biscuits into pieces about the size of almonds. Stir or fold these into the soft nougat preparation. This last operation has to be performed gently so that the biscuits don't crumble. The idea is that when the *torrone molle* is finally turned out and cut the little pieces of biscuit should look like whole almonds studding the chocolate mass.

Have ready either a turban mould, ie like a savarin or kugelhopf mould, or a simple loaf tin of 1 litre or 1¾ pint capacity, brushed with sweet almond oil. (This is to be bought from chemists. It's expensive but a little goes a long way and it's the best oil for brushing cake tins of all kinds.) Turn your prepared *torrone* into the tin, smooth it well down, cover it with a piece of foil or oiled parchment and leave it in the refrigerator until well-chilled, preferably overnight. It should then turn out easily.

I published this recipe in *Italian Food* (1954) and it has since been a good deal adapted in various ways. Some cooks think it's a good idea to add a spoonful or two of rum or whisky, others a little black coffee, others again a few drops of bitter almond essence. I'm not sure if any of these additions are real improvements, but if you do choose to try one or other of them, be very careful not to overdo either the liquid content or the flavouring.

CARROT CAKE (1)

Edwina Currie, MP
Under Secretary of
State for Health &
Social Security

2 eggs separated
8oz (225g) soft brown sugar
6oz (175g) Kraft Vitalite Sunflower
 Margarine, melted
2tbsp warm water
5oz (150g) wholemeal flour
1tsp baking powder
½tsp mixed spice
Pinch salt
1oz (25g) chopped walnuts
1oz (25g) sultanas
6oz (175g) grated carrots

Icing:
4oz (100g) Philadelphia cream cheese
4oz (100g) icing sugar
Zest of ½ lemon

Pre-heat oven to gas mark 5, 375°F (190°C). Grease and line the base of a 7in (18cm) cake tin or 2lb (1kg) loaf tin. Cream together the egg yolks, sugar, margarine and water. Sieve the dry ingredients into a bowl, add the nuts, sultanas and carrots, and mix well. Make a well in the centre and add the egg mixture. Stir well and mix. Whisk the egg whites until standing in soft peaks. Fold carefully into the cake mixture. Pour into the tin and bake in the pre-heated oven for 45–50 minutes, until a skewer inserted in the centre comes out clean. Cool on a wire rack.

To make the icing: cream together the Philadelphia and sieved icing sugar until soft and creamy, add the lemon zest and swirl over cake. Decorate with a little lemon or orange zest.

Microwave:
Bake in a 2lb (1kg) loaf-shaped container suitable for the microwave for 10 minutes. Leave to stand for 5 minutes before turning out on to a cooling rack. When cold, top with the icing.

Freezing:
Will freeze for up to 6 months.
Serves 10 (267 calories per serving)

TIPS: Keep the fat down; keep the fibre up; lots of fruit and vegetables.

DISLIKES: Washing up. We have a machine. My lovely mother-in-law took one look at me 15 years ago and gave me hers!

YOGURT CAKE

Baroness Ewart-Biggs (inspired by her daughter Henrietta)
Member of the
House of Lords

Use a small yogurt carton as a measure:
1 small carton of yogurt (any flavour)
1 measure caster sugar
1 measure sunflower oil
3 measures plain flour
2tsp baking powder
4 eggs
3tbsp jam (same flavour as the yogurt)
Icing sugar
Extra yogurt for the filling

Mix all the ingredients but the last three, either by hand or in a food processor. Place into a greased 8in (20cm) cake tin and bake in a moderate oven, gas mark 4, 350°F (180°C) for 40–45 minutes. When cool, cut in half and spread one half with the jam and extra yogurt. Put the other half on top and sprinkle with icing sugar.

MUESLI FINGERS

BBC Television's
Blue Peter

4oz (100g) honey or golden syrup
3oz (75g) brown sugar
4oz (100g) margarine
3oz (75g) wholemeal flour
8oz (225g) basic muesli with fruit and nuts

Put the honey or syrup into a saucepan*, add the brown sugar and margarine. Melt slowly over a low heat. Don't let the mixture boil, and make sure every grain of sugar has melted before you take it off the heat.

Mix the muesli and flour and then add to the liquid. Stir until thoroughly mixed up. You can also add some additional chopped nuts as an optional extra. Line a Swiss roll tin with kitchen foil, and grease well with margarine paper. Spread the mixture evenly over the tin. Bake for 30 minutes until golden brown in a pre-heated oven at gas mark 4, 350°F (180°C). Cut into fingers before it cools (watch out for your fingers, don't burn them!). Allow to cool slightly but remove from the tin whilst still warm.
Makes 20–24 fingers

*An easy method to weigh the golden syrup is to put your saucepan on the scales and add the syrup until it weighs an extra 100g.

DATE AND WALNUT SLICE

BBC Television's
Blue Peter

1oz (25g) margarine
3oz (75g) granulated sugar (white or brown)
1 egg
5oz (150g) dates, chopped
2oz (50g) walnuts, chopped
3oz (75g) self-raising flour

Melt the margarine in a saucepan over a gentle heat, then pour into a mixing bowl. Add the sugar and mix well together. Break the egg into a jug and beat well. Add the egg to the margarine and sugar and give the mixture a good stir before adding the chopped dates, chopped walnuts and the sieved flour. Stir and mix the ingredients together.

Line a 7in (18cm) baking tin with kitchen foil and grease, using a little butter or margarine. Spoon the mixture into the baking tin and spread evenly. Put the tin into a pre-heated oven, gas mark 4, 350°F (180°C) and bake for approximately 20 minutes. Leave to cool on a wire rack. When cool – turn cake out and cut in slices.

Swiss-roll blowers in the Bernese Oberland.

RB.
Robert Buhler

DOROTHY CAKE

Jane Birt
Wife of John Birt,
Deputy Director-General
of the BBC

4 eggs
½ pint (300ml) double cream
12oz (350g) sugar
8oz (225g) self-raising flour
1tsp vanilla extract

Chocolate frosting:
3½oz (90g) unsweetened chocolate
2½oz (65g) butter
5oz (150g) icing sugar
2fl oz (65ml) milk
A drop vanilla extract

Break eggs in a bowl and beat until light and foamy (at least 5 minutes). Add the cream and beat another 5 minutes. Pour in sugar, continuing to beat well. Blend in the flour and vanilla. Bake in a well-greased tubular pan in a pre-heated oven, gas mark 6, 350°F (180°C) for 50 minutes, or in two 8in (20cm) cake tins for 30 minutes. Turn out the cake and allow to cool.

To make the chocolate frosting, melt the chocolate in a saucepan on a very low heat. Add butter and simmer for about a minute. Add the sugar, then the milk, stirring continuously. Let simmer for about 2 minutes and remove from heat. Stir in the drop of vanilla. Allow to cool before frosting the cake.

CARROT CAKE (2)

Baroness Falkender
Member of the House of Lords

4 eggs
2 cups sugar
1⅓ cups oil
2 cups flour
1tsp bicarbonate of soda
A few nuts
3 cups grated carrot
Pinch of cinnamon

Icing:
¾ packet icing sugar
2 packets Philadelphia cream cheese

Cream eggs and sugar. Add oil, then flour. Grate carrots and add to the mixture with nuts. Put mixture into two 7in (18cm) round tins. Cook for 1–2 hours at gas mark 2, 300°F (150°C). Mix cream cheese and icing sugar together and spread on cake.

TIPS: Always add an egg to pastry and never give up trying, even after the disasters.

LIKES: The smell – and I love making mince pies.

FRANKLIN

This & that

CAFÉ BRULÔT

Richard O'Sullivan
Actor

Orange peel
Brandy or rum
Cloves
1½tbsp sugar
Coffee

Pare two small strips of peel from an orange with a potato peeler and cut them into slithers, like matchsticks, with kitchen scissors. Put a couple of good-sized glasses of rum or brandy into a small saucepan, add a couple of cloves, the strips of orange, and the sugar. Bring to the boil. Reheat the coffee and pour it into the cups, leaving them half full; then set fire to the brandy mix and pour it slowly into the coffee cups, stirring at the same time.
Serves 2

WELSH RAREBIT

Rt Hon David Steel, MP

8oz (225g) fresh Cheddar cheese or
  Cheshire cheese
½tsp dry mustard
A little paprika
Few grains cayenne pepper
Salt
A little beer or stout
Hot buttered toast

Shred the cheese and put it in a double saucepan. Let it melt slowly over hot water kept just under boiling point. Add the mustard, paprika, cayenne and salt to taste, according to the needs of the cheese. Then stir in gradually as much beer as the cheese will absorb. The mixture should be smooth and velvety.
    Serve on hot buttered toast or hot toasted biscuits.
Serves 4

TIPS: If you want to ice a cake in a hurry: Take a pretty doily and position it over the top of the cake like a template. Sprinkle icing sugar all over, remove the doily, and *voilà*! a beautifully iced cake that took only seconds to do.

SCOTCH POACHED EGGS

Ruskin Spear RA
Artist

Take 2 slices of toast, well-toasted, and dip for a few seconds in a shallow bowl of Scotch. Butter the damp slices with ample butter and sprinkle hot fried breadcrumbs liberally. Serve with two poached free-range eggs. Drink any remaining Scotch whilst looking through the post.

A fully recommended recipe. My grandfather thrived on it till 104.

"Take two slices of toast, well toasted"

Ruskin Spear

> Dear Mr. Wogan,
>   I am compiling a recipe book which is to be sold in aid of the N.S.P.C.C., and would like you to contribute a recipe worthy of your international mega-celebrity status.
>   I can't believe that so many of our best known and loved stars' faces are regularly filled with such uninspiring fare as tinned tuna fish and bread and butter pudding.
>   Could you please send a recipe liberally filled with oysters, champagne, truffles, smoked salmon and Beluga caviar as befits someone of your wealth and prestige.
>   Yours sincerely, Anna Hunter.

CHIP BUTTIE

Terry Wogan

Take two thick slices of crusty white bread. Spread both slices liberally with plenty of butter. Fill with sizzling hot, freshly fried chips. Season to taste.
Eat immediately!!

DISLIKES: Having to stop eating when I have finished my own, and everybody else's meal.

CULINARY DISASTERS: Only when a *nid des oeufs de caille* I had ordered in a West End restaurant had a slightly disappointing crust.

AMERICAN BITE

Catherine Cookson
Writer

Since I am allergic to most foods my diet is very limited. For many years now I have 'existed' on this lunch, which I call my American Bite. Why? I don't know!

An apple thinly sliced, I mean thinly; some pieces of various cheeses, a few nuts, some large stoned raisins; if available, some cress; a thin slice of buttered wholemeal bread or corresponding biscuits; and a dessert spoon of brandy in half a glass of milk. The food, naturally, is eaten with the fingers!

SIR OSWALD MUESLI

Richard Stilgoe
Songwriter and entertainer

Muesli
Remains of last night's fruit salad

This is a way of getting children to eat breakfast. On top of their bowl of cereal, add a face made out of bits of old fruit – grapes or raisins for eyes, a peach slice for a mouth, a cherry for a nose – that sort of thing.

If the family disapproves of Sir Oswald Muesli, you can try David Frosties or Sir Shreddie Laker.

Barry Fantoni

116

THE PERFECT LUNCH FOR ELDERLY AUTHORS

Frank Muir
Writer and raconteur

Take one slice of bread from a new loaf not more than three hours old (preferably Hovis but *not* wholemeal, which has bits of toffee in it).

Place in electric toaster and activate switch.

Turn the slice of bread every 20 seconds. First upside down, then back to front, then switch places with the slices and repeat. Wear gloves if fingers begin to blister.

When the toast is golden brown, the colour of a good potato crisp, remove and butter moderately. Use a country butter, slightly salted, at blood heat, and butter smoothly right up to the edges of the crusts.

Take a block of fresh, mild, Cheddar cheese, preferably from the West Country but some East Anglian cheeses are tolerable in an emergency. Carefully slice into pieces exactly three-sixteenths of an inch thick. Make a trial slice first and test thickness with calipers. Assemble the slices of cheese on the buttered surface of the toast in such a manner that the surface is exactly covered. In no circumstances must the cheese protrude beyond the perimeters of the toast. Use a sharp knife to trim off any surplus, working widdershins, ie in an anti-clockwise direction. Nor should gaps be left so that buttered toast is visible between the interstices of the pieces of cheese. Tweezers can be helpful in easing small wedges of cheese into the chinks.

Carefully spread on top of the cheese a half tablespoonful of marmalade. Homemade, of course, and rough cut. Try to obtain navel oranges grown on the hill area eight miles north of Cadiz; the zest has a fluted aftertaste which compliments the confident, almost jaunty, flavour of the juice.

Who says that man cannot make himself a simple meal?

MOVING SPAGHETTI

Roald Dahl
Writer

The dish that Mrs Twit cooked for Mr Twit:

Collect a tin full of earthworms from the garden. Put them on a plate. Cover them liberally with tomato ketchup and serve, preferably to your husband.
[You can read more about The Twits in Roald Dahl's deliciously funny children's story of the same name.]

Quentin Blake

Tea for Two by Mel Calman.

1. Boil the WATER. Very important.

2. Warm the TEAPOT.

3. Add a spoonful of TEA for each person.

4. Add the HOT WATER.

5. Serve with MILK or LEMON.

6. Hot buttered toast goes very well
   with TEA.

Lovely tea –
you must
give me
the
RECIPE...